HOW TO BE HEALTHY, WEALTHY
AND WISE

HOW
TO BE HEALTHY,
WEALTHY
AND WISE

by M. H. TESTER

THE AQUARIAN PRESS

This edition first published 1988
First published in 1972 by Psychic Press Ltd

British Library Cataloguing in Publication Data

Tester, M. H. (Maurice Harold),*1916-*
How to be healthy, wealthy and wise.
1. Personal success — Manuals
I. Title
158'.1

ISBN 0-85030-754-6

*The Aquarian Press is part of the Thorsons Publishing Group,
Wellingborough, Northamptonshire, NN8 2RQ England*

Printed in Great Britain by Richard Clay Limited,
Bungay, Suffolk

2 4 6 8 10 9 7 5 3

CONTENTS

INTRODUCTION

Early to bed,
Early to rise,
Makes a man healthy,
Wealthy and wise.
            Old saying.

WELL, it helps. A good night's sleep works wonders. You will start the day refreshed. Your body will have a chance to recuperate. And with that behind you, you have a distinct advantage. If you are feeling rested and refreshed many of the symptoms that have been ailing you will disappear or seem less worrying. If you are feeling better you will work better and think clearer. And that is as good a way to prosper as any. So there is a lot in this old saying.

But some people need less sleep than others. Some feel sluggish after a long night in bed. Others take to their beds too often as an escape from the world they feel is treating them badly. Going to bed early, having a full and refreshing night's sleep, and getting up whilst the day is new is fine. Try it. But most people in this complex society need more. What do you need?

Most of us need to be wanted, to be loved, to be appreciated. Most of us need success, freedom from money worries and a sense of fulfilment. Most of us need maturity so that when problems come along we can deal with them in a wise and balanced manner.

This book tells you how to achieve this. To the sick in body and heart it brings hope. To the failure it brings a way to success. To the ignorant it brings knowledge. Here is a blueprint for living.

But a blueprint is not enough. This book does not stop at giving you a plan. It explains what went wrong, how to correct it, why this design for living works, and promises you a life that is full, interesting, satisfying, vibrant, healthy and amazingly rewarding.

Who does he think he is?

I am glad you asked that question. I am a practising healer. For many years I have healed twenty to thirty people a week, ninety nine per cent of them suffering from medically incurable illnesses. Every week I have received and answered several dozen letters. I have seen the lame walk, the dumb sing, the bent straightened. My patients have taught me a lot. I can see now a pattern in the healing, and a method of avoiding illness. Many I have helped have gained more than health. They have become confident, serene and able to cope fully with the complexities of modern life.

If I can heal diseases of the mind and body, then why cannot I prevent them? I can. In place of illness I can offer health. Instead of ignorance I can give understanding. And with these forming the basis you can move on to a full, interesting and rewarding life.

Yes, but who *does* he think he is?

I am a nobody. When I am healing I am the least important person in the room. I merely fade as a personality and let the life force flow through me. I am the piano, not the pianist. I am the radio receiver, not the broadcaster. All I can do is to focus onto you the power that is already around you. There are many keys to this power. This book is one of them.

My earnest wish is that it turns in your hand.

M. H. TESTER

Chapter 1

WHY AM I ILL?

"WHY should this happen to me? I have always lived a good life. I have never done anybody any harm. Why should I be the one to be sick and ailing? Why me?"

Why, indeed?

Before we start analysing the causes of ill-health, let us sweep away one of the non-causes. Illness is not a punishment. There is no elderly gentleman with wings, in a long white nightshirt, marking it all down in a big book. Because of the superstitions they were taught in their childhood too many people harbour delusions of this nature.

They seem to think there is some sort of 'points' system. When the number against them reaches a pre-determined limit a finger is pointed at them. "John Jones. You now have the limit of points awarded for not going to church on Sunday, being cruel to your little sister, answering back your father at the table, and not saying your prayers every night." Then ... bingo! You've got measles!

No. Sickness is not a punishment. Often, though,

it is the effect of a cause for which you were responsible. You can worry yourself into a state where you get an ulcer. The cause is worry. The effect is the ulcer. Because you allowed yourself to have tension instead of tranquillity, stress instead of serenity, you made yourself ill. If it is a punishment it could be only you punishing yourself.

Suppose you were driving your car along the highway. You have a puncture when you are miles from anywhere. Fortunately there is a good spare wheel and a full tool kit. You change the wheel. Ten miles further down the road the wheel comes off because you did not tighten the nuts enough. The car is wrecked. Is this a punishment? No. It is cause and effect. This does not prevent your remorse. And if the accident hurt a passenger or another driver you could be deeply affected. You might even look for a cause outside yourself and superimpose a form of rationalised superstition. And from this you could make yourself ill.

Most illnesses are emotionally induced. The pain, discomfort and symptoms are all real enough. If you have an ulcer in the stomach, it hurts. The pain is caused by muscular contraction of the stomach lining. Yet it is now common knowledge that an ulcer is the result of stress. Most diseases are. I know this is a sweeping statement. You may be ill at this moment. Perhaps you are sitting up in a hospital bed suffering from what you know

is a purely functional ailment. Please do not resent
what I have written; it is true. Perhaps I had
better demonstrate it to you.

Your body is a complex mechanism. It houses
a structure that encompasses all the basics of
engineering. It is controlled by a computer of
such precision as to make its electronic counter-
parts look like steam-age machines. It never
ceases to amaze me that after many thousands of
years of research we know so little about its
workings. One thing we do know, though, is that
the fluids and secretions have to be very finely
balanced. A little too much blood sugar and you
have diabetes. Too few red corpuscles and you get
anaemia. A drop in blood pressure and you pass
out. An increase in the blood's clotting rate and
you get a thrombosis.

The mechanical balance is as sensitive as the
chemical. Contract the neck muscles when they
should be relaxed and you have a headache.
Induce a mild muscle sheath spasm and you get
fibrositis. For you to be in a state of full health
you need to have everything in your body in
balance. Let us look at a few reasons why this is
not so. In other words, let us look for the answer
to the question at the top of this chapter, " Why
should this happen to me?"

You are sitting in your favourite armchair
reading a book. You must have dozed off. Now

you are suddenly awake. It is dusk. The lights are not on. You are alone in the house. You can vaguely remember the noise that awoke you. The street light is casting a shadow through the open doorway and into the room. The shadow is that of a man with a gun. He is motionless, menacing you.

You are terrified. You are paralysed with fear. Your heart is pounding away. You are in a cold sweat. Your pulse rate soars as adrenalin is pumped into your bloodstream. Your blood clotting rate rushes up immediately as the body prepares to defend itself if you are wounded. The number of blood cells multiplies at a fantastic rate. Your blood pressure zooms from a static 130 to way over 230. The muscles that control the opening of the stomach cramp close as a safety measure. Your metabolism undergoes a rapid and amazing change as the controllers in your body hasten to defend it against attack.

A car turns into your roadway. Its headlights shine through the window. The room and the hall are for a moment brilliantly lit. The shadow changes shape. You let out a long sigh of relief as you see the tall figure is the hall stand, the gun is the handle of your walking stick. Even the noise is explained as the cat walks into the room, arches her back, and comes and rubs herself against your leg.

You laugh a little ruefully, turn on the lights, pour yourself a drink, light a cigarette, and return to your book. Your body's defences get the signal to stand down.

Quickly and without fuss the balances inside you are adjusted. Your heart rate drops to normal, your pulse is quiet again, your muscles relax, the blood stops manufacturing new cells at the fast rate, decreases its clotting ability, and lowers its pressure again to the norm. Your breathing becomes quiet. You stop sweating. The imbalance is gone.

For you this is an unusual event. You do not often sustain a fright of this magnitude. When you do, and your body is threatened, it is right that the mechanism can respond. It does so to protect you. You may be alive today because it has done so in your past.

But suppose it was a daily event, or even an hourly one. After all, it does not have to be fear that triggers off the defences. It could be anger. A business man sits down at his desk to go through his morning mail. The first letter is one from a firm he deals with repudiating a large order. He needs that order. He has borrowed from the bank against it. His horror is quickly reinforced by anger. "They can't do this to me. Who do they think they are? I'll show them. I'll sue them for every penny they have. Miss Jones, take a letter."

His face is suffused with rage. His heart is pounding away. The internal alarm bells are ringing. The body responds. Up goes the blood pressure, the clotting rate and all the other defence measures. He dictates his letter. He lights a cigar, drinks a cup of black coffee, sits back in his chair a little exhausted by his outburst.

He may do this several times a day; many days a month; hundreds of times a year; for a number of years. One day the clotting rate change is so overworked that it malfunctions. The blood retains its high clotting factor. A clot is formed and quickly builds. The flow of blood is blocked. The man dies from a thrombosis, or a blood vessel, weakened by constant changes of pressure, bursts at the sudden build up that his anger triggered off. The man dies of a haemorrhage.

This is a simple example of how an imbalance in the human body can kill. Often it does not kill. Instead the patient continues to live, but is ill. The stomach ulcer is a good example of this. A man's emotions set up an imbalance in the fluids of the stomach. The extra acidity attacks the lining of the stomach wall. He gets an ulcer. The adjoining muscles react to it. He is in pain.

The full extent of emotionally-induced illnesses is difficult to assess. One family doctor I spoke to put it as high as 95 per cent. I have seen the figures of a specialised clinic for gastric complaints.

This deals only with stomach cases sent by general practitioners. They kept detailed case histories. From these they calculated that 76 per cent of all their patients had gastric troubles which were emotionally induced. Practically all headaches, fatigue, constipation, dizziness, throat congestion and pains in the stomach, neck and back are emotionally induced.

One specialist published exact figures. He said that 90 per cent of tiredness, 70 per cent of constipation, 85 per cent of headaches, 90 per cent of lumps in the throat and 99.4 per cent of gas in the stomach were emotionally induced. Medical students are given a textbook of the diseases they have to understand during their training. There are about one thousand of these. One of them is as common as the whole of the other 999 put together. It is emotionally-induced illness.

You get ill, then, because the balance of your body is disturbed. You induce the imbalance. The result is one of the many symptoms with which we are so familiar, pain, sickness, stiffness of the joints, ulcers, growths, functional weaknesses, aches, tiredness, constipation and the terrible condition of just " feeling rotten."

The balance of your body is in the hands of a number of controllers. Perhaps the most important of these is the pituitary gland. This is situated at the base of the brain. It is no bigger than a pea.

It is the one that reacts fastest to the warnings. It does its job when it receives a triggering signal. You cannot make it work by consciously giving it instructions.

This also applies to all the other controllers. They do not react to orders. You can tell your fist to close and then to open. It obeys at once. But you cannot give a command to your heart. You cannot directly control your pulse, blood pressure, or the many other balancing factors. They will just not respond to a specific request. Nor will the glands that control them.

That is why when you are depressed you cannot talk yourself out of it. " Don't be a fool," you say. " Everything will come out all right in the end. There is really nothing to worry about. Something is sure to turn up." And you find you are just as depressed as ever. When you have a blinding headache you cannot cure it by telling your neck muscles to relax, any more than you can cure constipation by wishing.

" How does this apply to me?" you ask. " I do not often lose my temper. I am not frightened of anything. Yet I am ill." Anger and fear are the emotions that most obviously trigger off the body's reactions. But there are many others. Of these worry is the most common.

We live in troubled times. Since World War II there has been fighting going on continually somewhere. The world is not at peace. The build-up of massive and frightening arms keeps the economy of the Western world on a knife's edge. The threat of a new war that could destroy the world, as we know it, is a real one. We have invented weapons so powerful that our entire civilisation could be wiped out in twenty-four hours. We have at present neither the philosophical maturity to control them, nor the mental equipment to do so.

One of the particular terrors of the West is that the holocaust will be started by a computer launching a massive nuclear counter-attack against an act of aggression that is a human error and which a human could have corrected. The cults, like the hippies, that have attracted so many recruits from young people everywhere, exist because, as one twenty-year-old told me, " None of us expect to reach thirty." To millions there is one overriding worry. Will we survive?

To this can be added the worries that come from the materialistic and competitive commercial world in which we live. Under the continual pressure of advertising from magazines, news-papers and the ever-present television, we are persuaded, as no people has ever been before, to spend our money. Thus where the ownership of a car was once something to look forward to and to save for, now we have two- and three-car families.

And most of the cars are not paid for. Why save? Have it now. Pay later.

Add to cars all the consumer durables that we seem to need, like the television sets in colour, refrigerators, central heating, washing machines, new clothes every season, holidays abroad, and the untold number of status symbols that establish our place in society. So you get a drain on your financial resources that is capable of absorbing every increase in earning power. Financial worry is one of the most common of all.

To the worry of the future, add the one of today and you have a burden which the body's defences find it hard to repel. One more burden and they do not cope. And illness becomes serious. The burden that too many people add to worry about today and apprehension for the future is remorse for the past.

If I had £5 for every person who has started his history with a long and sorry tale of what wrongs he had suffered in the past, I could build and equip the finest healing clinic in the world. The past is useful. It teaches us where we went wrong. Any fool can profit from his successes. You are not a fool. You can profit from your mistakes. That, after all, is the best way to learn.

We all make mistakes. It is part of our personal education. A man who never made a mistake never made anything. But when we do so, we should remember clearly the lesson we learn, and apply it next time. Daily to go over the mistakes in your mind, to be continually sorry, eternally to relive the bad moments, and to harbour remorse or annoyance at what happened is adding a burden that will prove too much.

With a constant load of worry, trepidation and remorse your body is triggering the warning bells all the time. Instead of a single chime telling the body's defences to stand by, yours is a carillon. Your body has a permanent imbalance. You really are ill.

There are other emotions that cause imbalances. Whoever first listed the seven deadly sins was a sound psychiatrist. They are not sins against theology. They are sins against common sense. Any of them will make you ill. Any permutation of more than one will keep you ill. And any group of them can kill you. In case you cannot remember them all, they are pride, covetousness, lust, anger, gluttony, envy and sloth.

Now do not get the idea that you have to have the environment and the standard of living of Blackbeard the Pirate to push your body into ill-health. Let me give you a simple example of how emotionally-induced illness works.

A doctor in America had a very busy practice. He could not get an assistant. His nurse, on whom he relied heavily, had married and moved away.

He had too many patients. He was overworked.
The responsibilities of his practice were too much
for one man. He developed fibrositis.

The doctor was an intelligent man. He knew
that fibrositis of the shoulder was due to a muscle
sheath spasm and was nearly always emotionally
induced. Yet this knowledge was not enough to
clear the trouble. His shoulder continued to hurt.
All he could do was to take pain-killers and carry
on.

Now and again he did manage to take an after-
noon off. He went fishing. He noticed when he
was sitting on the banks of the lake with his rod
in his hand that he was then completely free of
pain. Yet before he reached his home the shoulder
was hurting as much as ever.

Being a scientifically-inclined person he decided
to do some personal research. He wanted to know
at what point on his journey to the lake the pain
stopped. So the next time he went fishing he kept
his mind on his right shoulder. It hurt badly. It
went on hurting as he drove along the highway.
He had purposely taken no pain-killers that day.
He wanted to be fully aware of the pain and the
moment when it stopped.

Suddenly it did. One moment it was giving
him hell; the next he was completely free of pain,
stiffness or any other symptom. He stopped the
car, turned it round and drove back to town. Less

than half a mile along the road the pain and stiffness came back with a spasm that almost made him sick.

He turned the car and drove towards the lake again. A few moments and the pain stopped. He drove up and down the highway until he located the precise spot where the pain stopped and started again. The road was empty. On either side were open fields. The only thing in sight was a small notice board. It said, " State boundary."

The doctor was licensed to practise medicine in his State. When he passed its boundary he was outside the area of his medical practice. The cause of his stress was removed. He felt fine. When he drove back again the mantle of responsibility and overwork fell on his shoulders. Subconsciously the point at which this happened was the State boundary. His fibrositis was emotionally induced.

Did that knowledge cure it? No, it did not. He was unable to change his attitude to his practice and the pain persisted. When he got a new nurse, and eventually an assistant, he started to go fishing more often. Only then did he get well. But he still got fibrositis twinges when he had a difficult case, or when the assistant was away on holiday.

Do not let the fact that the doctor could not control the fibrositis, even though he knew the cause, depress you. All I ask you to do for the moment is to accept that most diseases are caused by our emotions. Pause and take a long, cool look at your health problems. Try and analyse what caused them. Do not tell me you recognise that other people make themselves ill, but this does not apply to you.

It does. Even orthopaedic complaints can be emotionally induced. We do not look after our bodies. We take little or no exercise, eat the wrong food, maintain a poor level of personal hygiene and spend most of our time in an incompatible environment. Thus the body is never functioning at full efficiency.

Because we no longer ride horses, do no manual labour, travel everywhere sitting down and have almost given up walking, we develop poor tone in the big muscles of the lower back. Thus, prolonged standing, or any extra activity such as we might experience on the beach at holiday time, can induce a mild muscular ache in the lumbar region.

Because the back is weakened by lack of exercise it may be a little more serious than this. You may have a mildly prolapsed disc. This is a condition that often corrects itself without any treatment. If you were fit you would not have it, anyway. But if you are subject to emotional stresses you will put the big muscles in your lower back under constant tension. Then your spine will be distorted, the disc will be pushed to one side. It will press against the end of the sciatic nerve. This is a fat nerve that runs down each leg. Pressure on it produces a severe pain, known as sciatica. It can go right down the leg to the foot. If it gets really bad the foot can go numb.

The treatment is traction. During this the body is stretched on a rack so that the vertebrae can open and allow the disc to return to something like its normal position. If the condition persists you may eventually have to face an operation. It is called a laminectomy. It has a poor success rate. After this operation some patients still have the same or similar symptoms.

Slipped discs are getting quite common. They are classed as orthopaedic complaints. Yet most of them could be avoided. And once the initial minor prolapse occurred it could be kept as a mild ailment and quickly healed if there were no major muscular tension. The tension is the direct result of emotional stress.

As a healer I get a lot of patients with slipped discs. In fact I have become something of an expert at treating them. Some seem purely mechanical, like the man who twists too much when playing golf. But most are promoted from a mild to a serious ailment by the emotional state of the patient.

Even the man who puts out his disc playing

golf may not be the victim of a seemingly accidental ailment. I saw such a patient recently. He had a seven handicap, which made him a pretty good golfer. He swung at a difficult drive and felt his back ' click ' out. He came to me distorted, with one hip well out of true, his body bent, one leg shorter than the other, and in pain.

After I healed him he admitted that he had been under heavy stress at work. Some of his daily problems were getting him down. He had got into the habit of " taking my problems home with me." At the moment of the disastrous swing he was under tension instead of being relaxed. I explained to him how a violent twist of the torso at a time when the main back muscles were under tension could affect his spine.

There are hereditary weaknesses. There are congenital disabilities. There are ailments caused by war, motor accidents and forces seemingly outside our control. Of these I shall write later. For the moment I ask you to accept that the vast majority of illnesses are emotionally induced. You must accept this before starting the next chapter. If you cannot do so as a result of what I have written, please have a word with your family doctor. Ask him if he agrees that most diseases are emotionally-induced ones. Then read on.

Chapter 2

THE KEY TO GOOD HEALTH

A bounding good health is the foundation on which you can build a wonderful and rewarding life. It was Emerson who said in *The Conduct of Life,* " The first wealth is health."

Without good health you are working at a low capacity. The capabilities of your body and mind are reduced. Many opportunities are lost, or not even noticed. Socially and commercially you become a passenger. The good life seems to pass you by. When you are well you feel you can tackle anything. And you can. When you are ill the smallest task seems irksome and your problems are magnified into impossible obstacles.

Ill-health has become something we accept with resignation, like inflation and heavy taxation. You raise your eyes to heaven and say, " What have I done to deserve this?" An historian of political economy could trace for you the root cause of inflation and taxation.

The world has brought these scourges upon itself. The materialism that holds the West in its grip like a terrible disease is the biggest contributory factor. There are two others. They are the fantastically expensive cost of maintaining a global defensive system, and the fallacy, harboured by many, that they can get something for nothing.

It may be that you can do little to correct these conditions, although sooner or later you will have to try. But there is no need to accept ill-health with the same equanimity. *You* can do something about *yourself*. I am placing into your hands the key to abounding good health. Hold it there. Feel the power it gives you. Let me explain how to turn it.

As I have told you, most illnesses are emotionally induced. The controllers in your body alter the balance when they receive a signal. They do not react to a conscious demand. They are not programmed to do so. They will react only when a specific coded signal is received. That signal is your attitude.

When you adopt an attitude of fear the controllers react fast. The change in your metabolism from rest to roaring defence takes only a few moments. It is the same when you lose your temper. You may have seen this in somebody else. The " flare up " seems to happen in the twinkling of an eye, except that nobody's eyes are twinkling. One moment a man seems calm enough. A second later he is in a roaring rage. A chance remark or a specific insult (or even an imagined one) triggers off a paroxysm of rage. It happens frighteningly fast. The speed with which the body reacts is astonishing.

I came across such a case recently. A man was very much in love with his wife. She was a beautiful girl and his whole life centred around her. She was also shallow and foolish. One day she ran away with another man. In a note she said she had gone for good. Her husband had, up to that moment, been a man of good health, suntanned, robust and full of vitality. When he read the letter he just collapsed.

He was taken into hospital. There were almost too many symptoms to record on his chart. He had violent stomach cramp. He could not eat anything without the most virulent indigestion pains. Even a sip of water produced agony. He had to be fed through a tube. He had violent head pains. His temperature soared to 104 and stayed there. His blood pressure rose from his norm of 135 to 240. He could not control his bowels or his bladder. His skin developed a rash. He wanted to die and he nearly did.

This man had been subjected to a shock. The emotion generated by his wife leaving him triggered off such a massive imbalance that it nearly killed him. The reaction was immediate. He went from full and robust good health to being a very sick man in about 15 seconds. That is as fast as an imbalance can operate.

As quickly as you can be made ill by shock, or by any bad emotion, so you can be made well.

A girl comes home to her flat after a long day at work. She is tired by a job she dislikes and which offers little change from a drab routine. The journey has been especially irritating and uncomfortable. She plans to soak in a hot bath, to have a simple meal and to go to bed early.

Then the telephone rings. It is a boy friend to whom she is attracted. He has tickets for a concert where some of her favourite show-business personalities will appear. Afterwards he wants to go to a party and meet some of them. He will call for her in half an hour. When he arrives she is dressed smartly, newly made up, well groomed and sparkling with anticipation. The concert is a tremendous success. At the party one of her favourite stars dances with her. The party goes on till two in the morning. She arrives home feeling exhilarated. She says she could have danced all night. What happened?

What happened to the tired-out office worker? What happened to the girl in the wrapper who was going to soak in a bath and go to bed early because she did not have the energy to do anything else? How did Cinderella get the energy to go to the ball?

All that happened was that her attitude changed. One moment she was expressing tiredness, disgruntlement, lack of hope and dissatisfaction. Then a telephone call transformed these feelings into excitement, anticipation and pleasure. Her attitude was affecting her body's controllers. They were getting the message that she needed rest, she was worn out. They responded by slowing down her metabolism. They induced the condition in which after a hot bath and a simple meal she would sleep.

Then her outlook changed. She became suffused with enthusiasm. She was going places, doing things, enjoying herself. She needed energy, strength, endurance, a smile and a sparkle. Her emotions were now calling for a different set of bodily conditions. Immediately the tiredness was swept away. In its place was energy.

The coded signal that the controllers in our bodies react to is our attitude. This is the key.

YOUR BODY REACTS TO YOUR ATTITUDE.

This is not a theory. It is a clinically-proven fact. Your body swiftly reacts to your attitude. Bad news can make you ill. Good news can make you well. A telegram telling you that the company in which you invested your life savings had gone into liquidation could make you very ill. A similar piece of paper with the news that you had won a prize in a lottery and that you were now rich would make you feel wonderful.

Imagine standing in the hallway with the telegram in your hand. The first one with the bad news would get an immediate reaction. It would hit you in the pit of the stomach. You would feel sick. Your legs would seem weak. You would have to sit down. You would read the telegram again and look sightlessly in front of you. You might even be sick. But when you receive the good news you feel elated. You jump for joy. You laugh outright. Everything, including your body, feels fine.

Bad emotions create an imbalance in the body. Good emotions bring the body back into balance, and hold it there. An imbalance brings ill-health. A balance brings good health.

" That is all very well," you say. " But I cannot expect to get a telegram every day telling me I have won a fortune." You do not have to. You do not have to change anything in your life. *All you have to do is to change your attitude to it*. Let us get this quite clear, for it is important. I am not asking you to be brave in the face of adversity. I am not asking you to keep a stiff upper lip. I am not denigrating your particular problems. Nor am I saying that your life is all a bowl of cherries. I will assume that you have as many problems as most people. There is an Arab proverb about every man thinking his fleas are gazelles. May be yours are great big ones.

I have given you the key to good health. With good health your problems will seem less. You might even start to solve some of them. The other Arab proverb I particularly like is, " He who has health has hope, and he who has hope has everything." So let us assume that you are not at this moment enjoying full, robust good health, and that, apart from any other problems you might have, this is one you would dearly like to solve. I have given you the key. The key was:

YOUR BODY REACTS TO YOUR ATTITUDE.

I am now going to show you how to turn that key. If I have learned little in my life, there is one thing that makes the rest of my ignorance seem unimportant. The way to turn this key is one of the most important things in the world.

The emotions that make you ill are the bad ones. These are worry, anger, avarice, envy, intolerance, greed, lust, pride, covetousness, hate and fear. It is quite a list. Any one, or permutations of more than one, will make you ill, keep you ill, and even kill you. Any one can create an imbalance that will produce pain, disease and the most terrible symptoms. These are the emotions that make you sick.

The treatment of these bad emotions by the use of drugs is one of the social problems of our society. In Great Britain in one year the number of prescriptions for barbiturates, tranquillisers and analgesics amounts to over 45 millions. Perhaps I had better give you that in figures. Last year our doctors made out over 45,000,000 prescriptions for drugs to reduce emotional stress. In addition there are the thousands of minor drugs that are attainable without prescription, and the most common drug of all, alcohol.

None of these prescriptions would be necessary if everybody was able to change their attitude. You can change yours. I will show you how when I tell you how to turn the key. You will then be able to replace your bad emotions with good ones —replace aggressiveness with gentleness, anger with serenity, hostility with love, and intolerance with understanding.

These attitudes will bring your body into harmonious balance. They will do it as quickly and efficiently as the bad ones create an imbalance. Now I am not asking you to undertake a whole personality change. You may be well established in your ways. You may feel that at your age you cannot suddenly alter your attitudes. I accept this

... for the moment. Please be patient. Take it step by step.

Here is the way to turn the key. This is the secret. Your body will react to an attitude even if simulated. This is so important that you must read it again.

YOUR BODY WILL REACT TO AN ATTITUDE EVEN IF IT IS SIMULATED.

Remember what you have learned so far. Your body's controllers react only to a signal. This signal is your attitude. They will react swiftly to a good attitude just as they do to a bad one. It does not matter to the controller if the attitude is real or imagined. It does not matter if it is felt or acted. It reacts just the same.

Do you realise the importance of this? It means that bounding good health is immediately available to you. All you have to do is to act the part of a happy person and you become happy. Act the part of a man who is tranquil and you become tranquil.

If you do not believe me try it. Go into your bathroom and lock the door. Stand in front of the mirror and act the part of a man who has just had wonderful good news. It does not matter if you do not believe in it. It does not matter if you are thinking inwardly that you look foolish. It does not matter what you feel. It is how you act that matters.

It is your attitude that controls your body's balance. It is not enough to go through the process of thinking that you have just received good news. This is not a mental exercise. It is purely a physical one. *You have to act*. It may be difficult at first. I did not say it was easy. Nothing worth doing is easy. But think of the reward when you succeed. This is the way to turn the key to robust good health.

If you will spend half an hour each morning acting the part of a happy man, then for the rest of the day you will be happy. If for half an hour a day you will act the part of a healthy man, then for the rest of the day you will be healthy. You will not just *feel* healthy. You will *be* well.

It may be that some of the symptoms will take a little while to clear. If you have been worrying all your life and you have an ulcer as a result, it may take a little time for it to fade. But meantime you will stop making any new ulcers. You will stop the emotionally-induced muscle contraction that is making the pain unbearable. You will start the process of regeneration.

Can this cure all diseases? No, it cannot. But it can cure those that are emotionally induced and that, remember, amounts to 95 per cent of all illnesses. I will deal with the rest later in this book.

What about infectious diseases? This system will *prevent* infection, and that is even more important. Have you ever wondered why some people always seem to catch colds and others never do?

One man will have several colds a year. If influenza is about he is sure to catch it. He spends half the winter coughing and sneezing, or wrapped up in front of the fire, with a glass of hot whisky and lemon. Another, subject to the same sources of infection, remains well, never takes a day off because he is sick, and goes through the whole winter without as much as a sniffle.

Why is this? Does the influenza virus sniff at one person and say to itself that this is a tasty morsel and I must dig in here and raise a large family? Does it have a lick of another and think him too salty or over sweet for his palate?

No, the answer is simple. One man has the bodily environment in which a virus can flourish. The other is hostile to the virus. A body in physical harmony, balanced and working smoothly and sweetly, is not a suitable environment for any self-respecting virus or germ. We all have the seeds of infection in us. In some the seeds flourish, in others they die.

A doctor in general practice may see several

patients each day. Many have infectious diseases.
The doctor very seldom catches one. He is too
busy. He adopts a simple hygienic routine. His
attitude to disease prevents infection since it is
an armour against it.

I am a practising healer. For many years I
have had patients passing through my hands nearly
every week. Many are seriously ill. Practically all
suffer from medically incurable diseases. I have
never caught an illness from one of these patients.

Once you have tried the half-hourly morning
routine, you will see how you can change the
balance of your body permanently, so that it is
in harmony, and is kept in that pleasant condition.
All you have to do is to act good attitudes at all
times. It does not matter, remember, if initially
you do not feel these good emotions. Just act
them. So that when somebody is rude to you, do
not respond with rudeness. Replace a bad attitude
with a good one. Be kind. When you hear something that makes you angry, stop, adjust your
attitude. Be gentle and understanding.

Try to radiate an atmosphere of calm, whatever
your immediate reaction. The advice to turn the
other cheek is a sound one, although it may be
difficult to follow. Do not envy anybody. You do
not know what price has been paid. Gradually
you will learn to remember to replace a bad
attitude with a good one. When you meet a

neighbour in the morning and he says, " Good morning, how are you?" reply:

" I am very well. In fact I am feeling fine. I never felt better in my life. This is a wonderful day." You will start to feel well. It will turn out to be a pretty good day for you.

Whatever you do, avoid anticipating anything bad. Supposing you had replied: " I am feeling a little seedy. Frankly, I think I am sickening for something. Maybe it will only be a cold." Then be assured you will get ill, and soon.

The case I wrote about earlier of the man who had a complete physical breakdown because his wife left him is typical of many. You can shock your system into an immediate imbalance. You can just as easily create a balance and make yourself well. You can demonstrate this easily next time you get upset.

Perhaps you are upset at this moment. Maybe you have a lot of worries, or something or somebody has upset you. If you are feeling any stress let us cure it right now. Go into a quiet room where you will not be disturbed for a few minutes. Take off your jacket, loosen your tie and collar, undo your belt, kick off your shoes. If you are a woman remove or undo any restricting or tight garments. Pull the curtains so that the room is dim. Bright light is stimulating and this is not wanted. Sit in a comfortable chair. Link your hands. Cross your ankles. Close your eyes. Let your eyeballs slowly drift upwards. Do not force them. Let them drift. This is the position they take when you are enjoying dreamless sleep.

Now take slow, easy breaths. Breathe deeply and slowly and let your breath out fully. Pause before taking another slow, deep breath. Keep this up for only five minutes. At the end of that time, dress and return to whatever you were doing. You will feel relaxed and refreshed. Repeat whenever necessary.

This prescription is simple. All you have done is to adopt the attitude of a serene person, your eyeballs at rest, your body at ease, your breathing slow and unexcited. This is the attitude of relaxation. The controllers have immediately responded. The defences are stood down. The body is restored to a harmonious balance. You feel relaxed and refreshed.

After a few tries you will not need that quiet, darkened room. You will be able to carry out this simple exercise in attitudes in the train, office, or even in your parked car. The change in your state of health will amaze and delight you.

The body is a self-healing mechanism. All surgery and nearly all orthodox medicine is based on this fact. When a surgeon operates he does so with the safe knowledge that if he brings the cut parts of the body together, and holds them in position, they will heal. If the body was unable to heal itself, surgery would not exist.

This is true of medicine. Most ailments are treated by putting the patient to bed, removing as many causes of stress as possible, keeping him warm and relaxed, and letting his body heal itself. The doctor may prescribe drugs to ease the symptoms, or some to accelerate the natural process of the body. But without its self-healing properties he would be lost.

The self-healing function is a very powerful one. Once the cause of the illness is removed it works with astonishing speed. If you cut yourself you can see this happen. The body literally rushes defences to the site of the wound. It produces chemicals and materials to mend it just when and where they are needed. If you keep the wound clean and free from infection it mends in no time.

When you run a temperature it is the self-healing mechanism burning up the toxins. The bowels and kidneys are working at all times to get rid of waste products and impurities. And the ease with which you can make yourself sick demonstrates the speed with which the body rejects what is bad for it.

The factor that helps the self-healing programme quickest and most effectively is the restoration of the body to a balanced condition. It is then able to cope with the impurities and the defects like the well-oiled and maintained machine it wants to be. Let us sum up this chapter.

The key to health is that

YOUR BODY REACTS TO YOUR ATTITUDE.

You turn this key with the knowledge that

YOUR BODY WILL REACT TO AN ATTITUDE EVEN IF IT IS SIMULATED.

There are attitudes that produce illness. There are attitudes that produce health. Which ones you adopt is up to you. The body is a self-healing mechanism. It prefers to be healthy. To attain and maintain robust good health you must adopt a good attitude. If you cannot immediately do this, it is enough to act one. The more you act the good attitudes the better you will feel. Eventually, and soon, you will feel so well you will no longer be acting.

You now have one of the keys to health. You know how to use it. What you do with it is up to you.

Chapter 3

THE WORK OF A HEALER

I am a healer. I am not unique. There are several thousand healers registered with the National Federation of Spiritual Healers. Most of them heal the sick as a part-time occupation. They charge nothing, believing that the gift of healing should be free to all. They only heal part of the time because they have to earn a living in some other occupation. Some healers are full-time professionals. What is spiritual healing? How does it work? Will it help you?

Often I get referred to as a faith healer. I am not. I am a spiritual healer. There is a world of difference. Let us get this cleared up before we go on.

As I have explained, the body is a self-healing mechanism. Given the right psychological and physiological environment the body can heal itself of most things. The emotions are powerful stimuli to this healing process. Thus a sick person who is convinced he is going to get well has a much higher potential for doing just that than a man who believes he will not survive. Every doctor and every nurse knows that to instil into a patient the will to get well is an important step towards recovery. The faith healer believes it is the only step necessary. He works on the assumption that once he has been able to generate in a patient a strong emotional reaction orientated towards recovery, then the sick will get well. To do this he uses every trick he can. A faith healer is almost invariably a man of strong personality. He has to dominate the meeting with his patient. The sick person is made to feel that he is in the presence of a superior. The healer will use a whole gamut of rites, rituals and ceremonies to convince the patient, and to get an emotional reaction. He may wear a robe of an ecclesiastical nature. He may have an altar with sacred emblems, burn candles or incense, use the " sacred " music we have learned to associate with religion, speak in a chanting manner, even seem to be in some sort of trance state. The sick person is dropped into this pseudo religious environment, after being conditioned with tales of miraculous cures. He may be suffering from a medically incurable illness, be át the end of his tether, and emotionally in a condition verging on sheer desperation. A powerful faith healer operating in this induced and artificial atmosphere will generally manage to get an emotional response.

The faith healer gets results. If the illness is psychosomatic the likelihood of his success is higher. But there are a number of disadvantages to this method of healing. Often the healer imposes such control over the patient that he is well only when he is in his presence. When he goes home he feels ill again. Sometimes the " cure " lasts a few days and then the symptoms return. The patient is disillusioned and may give way to despair. But the chief objection to faith healing is that it may prevent a sick person getting to a spiritual healer who may be able to induce a full and permanent cure.

There are many faith healers operating throughout the world. They vary from the take-up-your-bed-and-walk-my-son sect to the Voodoo man in Haiti. One thing they have in common is that they all rely on the power of imagination. That they get results, and some people literally swear by them, is the measure of the extent to which their techniques stimulate the imagination. Perhaps the best known example of faith healing is Lourdes. There the whole pageantry and pomp of the Catholic Church is harnessed to getting an emotional response. They are very good at it. They have been practising for a long time. But the results are meagre. The total number of complete cures at Lourdes since they started totals no more than a hard working spiritual healer gets in a month.

I am not a faith healer. I am a spiritual healer. When a patient visits me he is shown into a quiet room. It may be my drawing room at home or my office in London. I am generally in my shirt sleeves because I generate a lot of heat when I heal. I sit the patient down and ask him to explain what ails him. He may have written to me for an appointment. Most people do. In his letter he may have given me a lot of details of his disease. But I invariably ask him to recite the full medical history right from the beginning. There is a reason for this which I will explain later.

The sick person finds himself in simple surroundings. There are no religious symbols. There are no candles, no incense, no sacred music, no special clothes, no altar, no effort to impress. In my home he is in the same environment as one is when visiting an old friend. In my office he is treated as he would be if he called on any professional consultant—his lawyer, for instance. I explain that I am a spiritual healer, that I have no orthodox medical qualifications, that I do this work voluntarily and without charge, that I can guarantee nothing, that he must treat the healing as an experiment among friends. If it works I am delighted. If it does not, then he has lost nothing. For those who wish to make a gesture after they have been healed there is an alms box in the hall. The money thus collected goes to charity.

To some this simple prosaic approach may seem lacking in warmth and compassion. But the patients that come to me for healing are all medically incurable. Nobody visits a healer for a cold in the head or measles. They come only after orthodox medical treatment has failed to cure the illness, or has made it worse, or because they have been told by their doctor that the disease is incurable and that they must " learn to live with it ". They come to me because they met a person who was cured by me and who recommends them. They come to me because they have read my book, " The Healing Touch," which tells them how I, myself, was healed and how I found I had the gift. They come to me because they have been sent.

Healing is a gift, like music or painting. And like other gifts it can be developed. It is a strange and wonderful gift. And a difficult one to explain. A gardener for whom plants grow well is said to have green fingers. Under his hands flowers bloom, trees blossom, and a garden becomes a thing of unusual beauty. He has a gift. Have you ever been in a hospital ward at night? The patients are restless, many are awake, the lights are dim but there is no tranquillity. Then a night nurse walks along the line of beds. She smoothes a pillow here, says a quiet word there, straightens and tucks in a sheet, smiles and disappears through the swing doors. She leaves behind her a ward still and quiet and tranquil. Few have this gift. Then there is the groom who can go into a stable which houses a highly nervous stallion. Nobody can get near him. He rears and kicks out. His ears are back and his eyes are wild. The groom walks towards him hissing through his teeth. He strokes his neck, whispers a few words, the horse is quiet. He allows himself to be led out and saddled. You can call it magnetism, know-how, technique. It is none of these. It is a gift that one man has that another lacks. The healer has a gift. In all humility I believe it is the greatest gift of them all.

When the sick person has finished his history I get him to take off his coat and make him comfortable on a stool. I then tell him to relax. I place my right hand on his forehead and the left on the nape of his neck. Before this I will have switched on the tape player. The music helps the patient to relax. I have fairly wide tastes in music. One day I may be using modern jazz, and then for a while I will have a run on the classics. In this position, in a simple and quiet room, with only the muted music as a background, I switch off my conscious mind. When I first started healing it used to take me ten to fifteen minutes to do this. I would stand there with my hands on the patient and feel myself drifting off and then pulling back again. Now, after years of practice, I can do it in a few seconds.

I cannot fully describe this feeling of attunement.
It is like a self-induced daydream, except that I
am not dreaming. My conscious mind is a blank.
I am in a very early state of trance, I suppose. I
am not fully aware of the room or the patient. In
fact when it is all over I am often surprised at
the appearance of the patient, whom I remember
only from another meeting, as it were.

As I stand in this state of attunement I feel a
strange power flowing through me. No concrete
words can do justice to this supremely abstract
feeling. I am not aware of time. I do not know
how long each healing moment lasts. Sometimes
there is vibration under my right hand. Sometimes there is heat. I myself get very hot at this
time. That is why I work with my tie loosened
and in my shirt sleeves. After this initial moment
my hands seem to move under their own volition
to other parts of the body. They do not always go
to the area of pain. In the case of a slipped disc,
for instance, the patient generally complains of
sciatica in the leg. My hands seek out the site of
the disc and fluctuate between there and the base
of the spine. This is where the pressure on the
sciatic nerve causes the pain in the leg. Always
the hands seem to gravitate to the source of the
illness, rather than the area where the symptoms
show.

A full healing session seldom takes more than

ten minutes. If a patient is to be healed then he will be in that time. Yet I give everybody half-an-hour if I can. This is because there is a period of settling in when the patient tells me his history, and a period of adjustment afterwards. This time is important. Although I say little before the healing act and keep quiet for a while after it, there is in the majority of cases an emotional release, sometimes startling in its intensity. Many of the men and women who receive healing cry after it. I have seen women racked with sobs, men turning away to hide the tears streaming down their faces. I had one case of a man of about fifty, a highly educated person, throwing himself at my feet sobbing his heart out on the carpet. I keep a large box of tissues handy. I need them several times a day. The people who do not give way to the emotional release feel it, nevertheless. They sit there quiet and serene, enrobed in a mantle of tranquillity.

Remember that this has been achieved in a prosaic atmosphere, without any religious symbolism, without very much discussion, without any of the empathy traditionally associated with emotional reactions.

I ask the patient if he feels better. Sometimes the healing is complete. The pain, the stiffness and the other symptoms have gone. He is healed. Sometimes the healing is not complete. The condition is much improved but not completely healed. The patient is given another appointment, generally in a week's time. At other times there is no appreciable change. The patient feels much stronger, more relaxed, a lot happier. But the condition that prompted his coming to me is still present. When I first started healing I used to be a little depressed when this happened. I was soon shown how wrong I was. Many of the sick who felt no improvement when they were with me reported that three or four days later they woke up feeling fine, and with the condition either fully or substantially healed. Others reported that although the immediate symptoms remained they felt very much stronger and able to cope with their problems. When I tell you what spiritual healing is and how it works these two types of cases will be easier to understand.

The life force is around us always. I call it the life force. You may call it cosmic energy, the Great White Spirit or God. The more I study this world of ours the more I stand amazed at the complexity of the design. Look at a million snow-flakes under a low power microscope. You will see that each is an intricate and fascinating pattern of crystals. Each is recognisable as a snowflake. Yet you cannot and will never find two the same. Look at the galaxy of the heavens and marvel at the complexity of those stars and the immensity of the concept. Consider the molecular structure of any common substance, the brilliance hidden in a diamond, the art in the form and colour of a simple wayside flower, the marvel of engineering that is the skeleton of every living thing. The fish in their private world in the sea, the birds soaring above us in the sky, night and day, the seasons, the tides, the superb complexity of the human brain, the perfection of a new born baby, great music, art, the architecture that man has created with the equipment he has been given. Look at it all. There is design everywhere. The whole of nature works because there are immutable laws of cause and effect. If there is a design, then there must have been a Designer. The design, the creation, the continual operation and evolution . . . all this requires power. The power is still here. It will be with us and around us and of us until the end of time. And this is the power that heals.

" Show it to me," you say. " Show me that I may see this power."

Rip Van Winkle slept for a hundred years. Suppose he awoke today and you came upon him. You said to him, " There is music around you." He replied, " Show me." From your pocket you take a transistor radio. " The music cannot be seen. It can be heard. It is around us now. We cannot see or hear or feel it. It is on a wavelength that you and I cannot receive. This is a transistor radio. It converts one wavelength to another so that we can hear. All I do is turn this knob. There. You *can* hear it."

I am a receiving set. I have the gift of healing. I can take in the life force and change it into a power that a sick patient can receive. I cannot show it to you any more than I can show you a radio wave. But the results I demonstrate many times a week. I cannot analyse the life force. I do not know what electricity is, either. But this does not stop me plugging in a heater when I am cold or switching on the light when I am in darkness. If I said I would not use electricity because I could not see it and I did not know what it was, I would be laughed at. I would sit in my cold dark room and be reviled by my neighbours. And rightly so. Let me continue the electricity comparison further.

There are three rooms in a building. They are occupied, but in darkness. The tenant of the first room asks the engineer for electric power. The engineer throws the switch. The power flows along the lines. But the woman in the first room is a fool. She has not put a bulb in the socket. She remains in darkness, complaining of her lot, cursing that nobody helps her. In the second room is a man. He, too, asks for power. He has anticipated his request being answered. There is a bulb

in the socket and the switch in the room is on.
As soon as the engineer throws the switch the
room is flooded with light. The man has received
and used the power. In the third room are a husband and wife. They, too, have asked for the
switch to be thrown. When it is, they, too, are
ready. But the man has studied the subject. He
measured the current that is flowing. He now
knows that it will do more than just light a bulb.
His bulb is in the socket all right, but he has also
plugged in a radio and is learning to speak French
and appreciate classical music, and his wife has
connected an electric sewing machine and is
making a new pair of curtains.

All three of these people have received the same
power. Yet they have reacted in different ways.
The engineer can do no more. He has done his
job and thrown the right switches. The current
is flowing towards those who asked for it. His task
is done. What the recipients of the power do with
it is up to them. But there is someone who can
help them. Perhaps the electricity company sends
out a man to see if the people in the rooms are
receiving the power correctly. He shows the first
woman how to plug in a bulb. She is sitting in the
light for the first time. To the man next door he
offers one or two accessories such as a heater to
keep him warm. To the married couple he gives
encouragement, a tape player with several

language courses, and patterns for making clothes on their sewing machine.

Come back to healing. The electric current is the life force. The healer is the engineer. The man the company sends round to help those who need it is a spirit guide.

Yes, there are spirit guides. Every healer knows the feeling of being brushed aside as someone seems to take over his body and use it. This does not happen with every healing act. The first time it happened to me it seemed very strange indeed, but not unnatural. Now I accept it as an important part of the healing process. It seems that when a man is chosen to heal and is given this great gift he does not have complete control of it. Maybe the power is too much for a mere human to have. With the power comes one or more guides. Their job is to help direct it, to see that it is used properly, and to apply it where it is needed. I have one particular guide who helps me with healing generally. It seems that he can call on a small band of specialists who understand diseases that need different treatment. One, I know, is a neurologist, another an orthopaedic physician, and so on. There are times when I can feel them around me. There are periods when I am quite unaware of them. The patient who feels little at the healing session but reports that he is so much better a few days later, has had a visit from one or more of my guides. They may find some subconscious opposition to the healing when the sick person calls on me. After all, many are taught that all healing that does not come through the Church comes from the devil. Although this is palpable nonsense, the orthodox indoctrination of young children goes deep. It may in adult life inhibit healing. Where a block is found the guides wait. They are not bound by time or distance as we are in this world. Perhaps three or four nights later the patient is in a sleep of a depth that is adequate for their purpose. With the resistance gone they can then direct the life force and the sick person wakes healed. This has happened so often that it no longer surprises me.

There is the case of the patient who seems to get no specific benefit from the healing, but who feels generally a little better. The guides are very sound diagnosticians. They know when a person is at a low ebb. Sometimes they know that a full injection of the life force would be such a shock that the sick person might react to it too emotionally. When this is their view, they restrict the power. The patient gets small doses of the healing force. It tones up his system. After a few visits he feels very much better generally. His whole metabolism is beginning to function on a more healthy level. When they are satisfied that this is so they release the restrictions, and the sick one is healed. When the patient tells his history I know the guides are listening.

There is one other kind of healing you should know about. This is called Absent Healing. When I first heard of it myself, I was a little sceptical. I shall not be surprised if you are. Because with absent healing the healer never meets the patient. The healing act takes place from a distance. Before you dismiss this as impossible reflect on what you do accept.

An athlete breasts the tape in a one thousand metre race in Mexico. He is photographed doing so by a television camera. The image is converted into electrical impulses. These impulses are fed into a portable transmitter. It sends them up an aerial and across country to a large receiving station. There the signals are monitored, amplified and sent on their way to a beam transmitter. This beams the impulses through the atmosphere, through space to an artificial satellite orbiting the Earth at a height of many hundred miles. The satellite bounces the signals it receives back to Earth at another place on the globe. The signals are received by a dish aerial, transformed into a modulation of lower amplitude, sent to a central receiving station, monitored and broadcast on an ultra high-frequency wavelength, picked up by the multi-aerial on the roof of your house, passed down a wire into the back of your television set, and are finally displayed on a glass tube in the form of a detailed high quality picture. The whole of this complex and seemingly miraculous chain of events presents the picture to you only a fraction of a second after it happens. To all effects you are seeing the athletic event when it actually occurs. The words appear on your screen, " live by satellite." You ignore them as you sit back to watch the next race, or miss them as you give your attention to opening another bottle of beer.

If you accept that human ingenuity can do this, why maintain that God cannot?

The healer gets a letter. The letter is from a sick person one hundred miles away. He writes that he is bedridden and cannot visit the healer. Yet he asks for help. The healer holds his letter in his hands. He seeks attunement just as if the patient were present. He visualises the condition of ill health, and then he drifts away. As with contact healing, a few moments suffice. The healer puts down the letter and turns to the next in his morning mail. The guides play a larger part in absent healing. They are aware, through the healer, of the identity and location of the patient. They apply the healing power to him, either at the time of the healing intercession or later when the sick person is more receptive. And it works. I get several dozen letters a week from people telling me they are healed. Patients who wrote a week or two ago to tell me they were bedridden come to my home to thank me and to ask for further strength. I know of healers who get not dozens but hundreds of letters. The total number of authenticated cures from absent healing in England alone runs into many thousands.

Absent healing works. But it is not as a result of prayer or wishful thinking. Healing is a positive and definite act on the part of the healer. He has to hold in his mind the identity of the patient and the cause of the illness. He has to seek attunement. The process is the same as in contact healing. Prayer is a great force. I do not deny it. All the healers I know are deeply aware of this. But healing does not depend on prayer. It relies on a conscious act on the part of a man gifted to do just that. In fact, prayer can sometimes be a hindrance.

I remember a little time ago being telephoned by a local woman we knew. She told us her daughter was ill and was threatening to take her life. As the girl lived in a village near my home I went to see her. She was happily married, had an attractive home and two fine little children. But she was a highly strung person, with a mother who was as bad as she, and lived in a highly charged emotional environment. She had a prolapsed disc in her neck. She wore a surgical collar. The condition had not responded to medical treatment. She was in constant pain. She had worked herself into such a condition that she felt she must " end it all!" When I was shown into the room she said, " What can you do? The vicar has held a healing service for me. If the church cannot help, what can you do?" I could not explain to her that the vicar was a kindly theologian with no more healing power than a pork butcher. Yes, I did give her healing. She is now very much better. But I doubt if she will ever be completely well as long as she lets her mother inhibit her life. What this story does point up, however, is the fact that prayer itself does not heal. If it did then the " Please, God, make me better " prayers that most sick people say would be enough.

The life force is around you at all times. A healer is able to focus this and to transform it into a vibration your body can receive. This stimulates the self-healing mechanism of the body. It restores the balances. The healing is sometimes immediate and seemingly miraculous. Sometimes it takes a while. Through the healer you are linked to this power. In the next chapter I am going to tell you more about this power and how you can plug yourself directly into it.

Chapter 4

PLUG YOURSELF INTO POWER

So far we have looked at two methods of getting and keeping well. The first consisted of altering your attitude, so that the controllers in your body are triggered to restore the balance. The second is to go to a healer and let him harness the life force to you. There is a third method open to you. That is to plug yourself directly into power.

If you are going to take any piece of electrical equipment and connect it to the mains you need to know something about it. You would not buy a new washing machine, for instance, take it home and plug it in without first reading and understanding the instruction book. You would want to know what sort of plug you needed, how to adjust it to the current in your house, if the voltage, or ampere and fusing were all correct. Then you would need to learn how to connect the water supply, whether it should be the hot, or cold, or both, how to connect the waste outlet, what knobs to turn and when. You would want to find out a great deal about an automatic washing machine before you operated it.

Your body is far more complex than a washing machine. It is the most complicated machine in the world. And the brain that controls it makes the most sophisticated computer look like a child's toy by comparison. So before you connect yourself to the power you need some instructions. Remember the body is more intricate and the power far stronger than any man-made machine.

The first thing you must understand is that your body is not you, nor is your brain. The real you is a spirit expressing itself through the body and the brain for its life in this world. You are not a body and a brain with a spirit. You are a spirit using a body and a brain. The body is merely a vehicle (and the brain its computer) that you are utilising for the moment. Initially you may not find it easy to accept this. But it is true. The evidence for individual survival after death is overwhelming. Only the body and the brain die. The spirit is immortal.

When you reach the end of life here you will cast off your body like a worn overcoat. Then you will return to the spirit world from which you originally came. It may be that at the moment you cannot accept this truth. No matter. Keep an open mind and read on. But while you are doing so, pause from time to time and consider. Consider your own immortality. You are immortal. You will survive this life. Get used to the idea. It changes everything!

Your life in this world is an education. It was not picked out for you. You chose it yourself. A long time ago you, in your spirit form, went through a period of critical self-analysis. You had your guides to help you. They are spirit people more evolved than you, who have elected to help you. When you had all taken a long, cool look at your progress, you decided that your spiritual evolution would be aided by a course of education in this world. Maybe you needed more compassion, love or tolerance, or a little more suffering so that you could understand the problems of others. Whatever the course of instruction you needed, you felt you could find it here.

Then one day a man and a woman came together. A seed was fertilised. Your awareness of the fuller life was temporarily erased. You entered that seed and in the fullness of time were born into this world. Your pre-natal memory would be restored only when you returned to the spirit world. But in the course of your life you would sometimes be aware of a previous existence.

The life you have chosen is an education. Like most courses it has a syllabus. The length of the course is known. The terms are all noted down, as are the holidays. But what you do is up to you. Within this general framework you have free will.

As you progress through your course you are set tests, to see how you are getting on. You may find some of these tests irksome. You may find some discouraging. Do not be downhearted. The tests are necessary. What you do with the problems that are set is what matters.

Patients often begin their histories by telling me they have had a worrying life. This is untrue. They have, perhaps, been set some tests. They have failed them. That is shown by the worry. Sometimes, however, you do need help. If you were at university you would have access to your tutor. You have one or more tutors on this course, too. They are your guides. They are the same ones who helped you choose the course. They will see you through it. When you need help you can get in touch with them.

We have been brought up to believe a lot of fairy tales about the gods. Apart from the stories in the Bible we were taught classical mythology. We expect that if we receive a spirit communication there must be one or more of the phenomena we associate with this kind of act.

Thus a burning bush, a chariot coming down from heaven, a burst of heavenly music, a change of temperature, a strange light, thunderbolts, lightning, a great voice sounding from the mountain top—these we would respect. And if none of these things happen we are disappointed. Yet spirit communication is possible. You can open your ears if you will only open your mind.

Try an experiment. Let us suppose you have a problem. You have done your best. It remains unsolved. It does not matter what kind of problem it is, as long as it is not a selfish one. If your problem is that you want a Rolls Royce, or to win a lot of money in the football pools, or to have a bigger house, or some other purely material gain, this experiment will not work. There are other ways of gaining financial success. I am going to tell you of these later. For the moment let us take a problem unconnected with material gain. But it is a real one. It is troubling you. You have done what you can. You cannot see an answer. You need help.

You are going to extend the technique you practised in Chapter 2. Go into a room where you will be uninterrupted. Pull the curtains so that the room is dim. Remember bright light is stimulating. Take off your coat. Undo your tie and your collar. Loosen your belt. Kick off your shoes. Sit in a comfortable chair. Relax.

Then state your problem. Aloud, and in simple terms, tell, as if to a friend, what your problem is. Then explain you have done your best and you are now handing the problem over to them for attention.

Link your hands and cross your ankles. In this comfortable position in your dim, quiet room, close your eyes. Let your eyeballs drift upwards. Do not force them. Release the muscles around the eyes and let them drift. When you are enjoying dreamless sleep this is the position your eyes adopt. Let them drift upwards. So far this is identical with your relaxing exercise.

Then clear your mind. When you have had a lot of practice you will be able to do this at will. But initially it is difficult. A useful alternative is to replace your active thoughts with one large passive one. Think of a white rose. This means nothing in your life. It has no connection with the environment of your problem. (N.B. If you are a white rose grower and business is terrible, think of a white gardenia.)

Whenever you find your problem, or anything connected with your daily environment intruding into your thoughts, concentrate on a white rose. Fill your mind with the picture of it. Let nothing else intrude.

Gradually you will find your whole body relaxing. You may sit for ten minutes or more in this comfortable and almost floating state. You may even drop off into a light sleep. When you come to, stand up, stretch your arms up high.

Get dressed, drink a glass of cold water. You will feel unusually refreshed.

What you have done is open yourself to your guides. Your barriers were down. Your inhibitions were dormant. Your guides were able to commune with you. This is an important word. What you can do as often as you wish is to commune with your guides. You do not need communication. You have communion.

You feel better. You are more relaxed. You have given the problem to somebody else for attention. You have plugged in to the greatest power in this and every other world. You will get help. Often help takes a different form from what you anticipated.

You were trying to wade through a problem. In a few days the problem fades away as a man changes his mind. Or the solution is there in your mind whole and in full detail. Suddenly, without thinking about it, you know what to do and how to do it. Or something happens that changes the whole pattern and the problem ceases to exist.

What you must avoid is the temptation to tell the guides what to do. This is often difficult to resist. You may have troubles that are basically money ones. It would be easy to ask for the name of the winner of the 3.30 at Epsom. You may be troubled by a neighbour. It would be easy to ask for him to move away. Your answers to the problems are seldom the right ones. Do not tell them what to do. Just state your problem clearly and simply. Ask for help. Then go into your quiet room and let them come through to you.

All my major problems are dealt with this way. I invariably get the help I need. Sometimes it takes an unusual form, as when I wrote my first book, *The Healing Touch*.

I had been healing for a few years. After listening to the stories of hundreds of sick people I began to see a pattern. Most of them needed education rather than healing. I had a time when I was continually getting patients ill from grief. They were not imaginary diseases. These people were really sick, in pain and functionally disabled. Yet the factor that had upset the balance of their bodies was grief.

Now I knew that we survive death. Death is a great change. It is a time when the course in the university of life is over. We graduate to a greater, fuller life. It certainly should not be a time for misery. The rites and rituals of death in the Western world are barbaric, cruel and downright ridiculous.

I got tired of explaining all this to people made ill by their grief. I decided to write it down. I sat at my portable typewriter one evening and wrote, *The Bewildered Man's Guide to Death*. I did not have to think. It just came. My hands seemed to

type it on their own. But before I opened the typewriter cover I sat for a quiet moment. I have no
doubt that the guides wrote it for me.

When it was finished I put it into an envelope
and sent it to Maurice Barbanell, Editor of *Two
Worlds*. It was too long for a magazine article
and too short for a book. I asked him what I could
do with it. His reply was brief and to the point.
He printed it in full in *Two Worlds,* leaving out
some regular features to do so.

The response was amazing. Thousands, it seems,
had needed a guide to death. There were lots of
books on how to be born. Gynaecology was well
documented. There were lots of books on how
to live. That is what philosophy is all about. But
it seemed nobody had written on how to die. It
was reprinted as a slim booklet.

In London's Great Queen Street are the Con-
naught Rooms, with a fine restaurant and a
number of banqueting rooms. A publisher was
attending a formal luncheon in one of them. At
the end of it he walked across the road for a
breath of fresh air. He found himself looking into
the window of the Psychic News Bookshop.
Displayed in front was my booklet. He was
intrigued with the title. He bought a copy.

Next day he got in touch with me and suggested
I write a book. We had a number of meetings. He
seemed fascinated by my story of how I was cured

by a medium and came to do healing. He suggested I write a book that was part autobiographical, telling my story. The rest should be devoted to healing and to the philosophy that makes death so natural, acceptable and even exciting.

I wrote the book. When it was finished I sent him my manuscripts. He kept it a long time. Then he sent it back. He said it was excellent. He liked it very much. But he had just acquired a partner who would eventually control and take over the publishing business. He had strong religious prejudices. He refused to publish it.

It took me a long time to write that book. And here I was with a rejection slip from the very publisher who had suggested I write it. I had a problem. It was not the kind of book you could hawk around. I needed a sympathetic and mature publisher. How could I find one?

Well, when I have a problem I cannot solve I ask for help. I went into my quiet room and meditated. Soon I felt relaxed, refreshed, but no wiser. A few days later I found myself lunching with the director of a publishing company. I sent him my manuscript. *The Healing Touch* was published simultaneously in London and New York. It has been a great success and helped many people. I still get 50 or 60 letters a week from those who have read it and felt compelled to write to me.

You, too, can get help in this way. Your guides use the life force as you use electricity. They apply it often in a manner you could not anticipate. That is because you do not fully understand it. You never will, not in this world, at least.

Each of us is at a different stage of spiritual evolution. There may be two babies born at the same moment. One may be at an early stage of spiritual life, the other at an advanced one. One may grow up brutal, unaware, a slaughterman at an abattoir. The other may become a great philosopher, a sage.

You are at a different stage from your fellows. You may be ahead or behind them. No matter. It is what you do with your knowledge that counts. But if you are going to plug into this enormous power you really should read a little about it. So please finish this chapter, even if you do not fully accept what I write.

The quiet moment gives you an opportunity to commune with your guides, to receive the help they feel is needed and to have the life force flowing through you. The relaxation you feel afterwards is refreshing. Once you see this system to solve your problems you will be able to do away with worry. And worry is the major cause of imbalance in your body. Not only will tensions go and the balances be restored, but you will feel a great sense of regeneration. You will feel great.

If you practise the quiet moment every day, and at the same time adopt healthy attitudes, you will soon become well and enjoy radiant, bounding good health. As you become more expert you will be able to dispense with some of the tricks you needed initially. The mental concept of a white rose will no longer be necessary. You will be able to clear your mind of your problems and your daily environment whenever you wish. You will be able to switch out of your surroundings and have your quiet moment in your office, train, or in your parked car. You can plug in anywhere and at any time.

Your guides will help you whenever you ask for help unselfishly. They will connect the power, throw the switches, tune in to the source of it all. What are you going to do with the full, pulsating life that will become yours?

You are here, remember, to lead a life that will help your spiritual evolution. The key to spiritual maturity is service to others. When the end of your earthly life is near you may wonder if it has been successful.

What criterion will you apply? Will you add up your money and consider you have been a success if it is a large total? Will you look at your business and think yourself successful if it is a bigger one than when you took it over? What standard of success will you apply? Is a Rolls-Royce, a large house, a swimming pool, a collection of status symbols enough?

There is only one true standard. *Is the world a better place because of me?* What have I done to improve the lot of my fellows? The extent to which you are able to apply this criterion to your life is the measure of your success and of your spiritual maturity. Once you recognise this standard and apply it, many of your everyday problems take on a true perspective. When your time comes to undergo the big change we call death do not be afraid. You will find a great lessening of tension. All pain and discomfort disappear. You will find yourself drifting above your body. Connecting you to the sick and almost useless earthly body is a silver cord. It pulses slowly. Gradually it fades. Then it is gone. The face of your now useless corpse is covered with a sheet.

You, the real you, drift upwards through a silver mist. You find yourself moving forward. Your guides greet you and take you by the hand. You meet those you loved in this life and who had gone on ahead. The mist lifts and you are in a brilliant, colourful and happy place. You have graduated.

Time passes. It cannot be measured by our dimensions. It may be a few weeks, or thousands of years. Your guides greet you one day with serious eyes. You sit down together in silence. And in silence the life you have led is enacted before you, as if on a television screen. Everything you did, good, bad or silly, is there. You sit quietly and see and remember. Nothing can be hidden. You cannot hide from yourself.

When it is over you analyse it. Did you learn what you were sent to be taught? What should be the next step? Do you come back to this world for another life to give you the lessons you still need? Or do you go to a higher plane where spiritual education is more advanced?

Perhaps you elect to help somebody through this life and become a guide. Perhaps you feel you must go back and try again. If this is your decision, it is yours and yours alone. The guides will advise and help, but the decision is yours.

Then you choose a life that will give you the form of education you need. You wait until the moment is ripe. You say "au revoir" to your friends whom you will not see for a while. Your pre-natal memory is erased again.

Again, as a man and a woman come together, the seed is fertilised and you begin a new life. Maybe the body you are to occupy this time will be that of a genius or a moron, an athlete or a cripple, a famous man or a nonentity. It does not matter. It is what you do with what you have that counts.

You may feel I have strayed a little way from

the subject of this chapter. Not so. This part of
my book is about the power you can tap. It is
right that you need to know something about the
source of that power, and what you are supposed
to do with it.

There is one other method of finding out. You
may be satisfied only by direct communication.
Perhaps you are one of those people who need
something very fully demonstrated before you can
accept it. I do not condemn this. When people ask
me what they should believe I tell them: " Believe
only what makes common sense to you. Accept
nothing that cannot be proven." Those are big
words. But I suggest that what I have written so
far makes sense.

The proof of spiritual healing is that it works.
I have never advertised for patients. They come
because somebody who was healed recommends
a sick person to me. The proof of healing is in
the thousands of well people who were ill, and
the fact that over a thousand new patients a year
are sent to me.

The proof that the quiet moment works can
be ascertained very simply. Try it. The proof that
a change of attitude can make you well is there
in masses of clinical records. But you do not have
to accept them. Try it yourself. Do not believe it
unless it works. I would not be writing this if it
were not true. I have nothing to gain. I enjoy

bounding, robust, good health. I feel fine. It is you who are seeking health.

If you cannot at the moment accept survival of death, then do not worry about it. The evidence is strong. But you need personal proof. Quite right, too. What are you doing to get it? After all, you should be doing something. I say YOU ARE IMMORTAL. This, surely, is the most important thing about yourself that you could possibly be told.

It means YOU WILL NOT DIE. YOU WILL LIVE FOREVER. Is not this important? Should you not find out if I am right? Maybe you do nothing because you do not know what to do. Perhaps I can help you.

I have the healing gift. This means I can link with the spirit world. The guides direct the life force that flows through me to the sick person. I act as a medium. In fact I am a medium, a healing one. There are other people who have the gift of opening themselves to the spirit world. They do so not to have the life force flow through them, but to become a channel for communication.

I am a channel for healing. They are channels for knowledge. But we are all mediums. The conventional idea of a medium is faulty. Some think of him as a strange, moody person, sitting in a dark room surrounded by floating trumpets, weird voices, gongs, moving wine glasses, crystal balls, tarot cards and knockings on the table.

The real picture is commonplace by comparison. Most mediums sit in a plain, small room in ordinary room light. Some like a dim light because, as I have said before, brightness is stimulating to the senses. They vary in size, sex, outward appearance and education as much as any random collection of people can differ.

The gift of mediumship can be conferred on a small, poor woman or a big, wealthy man. I know of no common denominator other than their mediumship and desire to serve their fellows.

Many sit for nothing. Some charge a small fee. When you visit a medium you generally find yourself talking to an understanding, sympathetic person in a simple room. Sometimes the medium may go into a trance, but this is not often necessary. Sometimes nothing happens. Sometimes you get results that surprise you.

I shall never forget the first time I sat with a medium. It was Estelle Roberts, one of the great mediums of her day. She lived in a pleasant home at Esher, a few miles south of London. We sat in a small sitting room. The curtains were not drawn. The light was normal.

My wife and I were not known to her. She was in an armchair. She spoke in a natural voice about us. Sometimes she paused as if listening to a voice we could not hear. What she told us that day was very personal. One thing sticks in my memory. It concerned a war incident that happened in 1941. I had not mentioned it to a soul. My wife knew nothing about it. I had not consciously thought about it for many years.

A young fellow officer had been killed. He was engaged in an operation that should have involved me. He had taken my place at the last moment. I stayed safely at base. He never returned. I felt he had died for me and that I should have been the one to go. He had been close to me. We had been together throughout our training. I was very fond of him.

Estelle Roberts described him, his uniform, the manner of his death, and then said he had a message for me. He said I was not to have remorse. It had not been my time to go. It was his. It had been meant that way. I was in no way to blame.

This proved survival of death to me as no more dramatic demonstration could have done. Since then I have had many proofs. I have now gone beyond the realm of belief into the area of knowledge. You really ought to find out for yourself. It is much too important a matter to remain in ignorance about. It is also too important for sitting on the fence. Jump right in, the water's fine.

Let us sum up what we have learned so far. There are three ways open to you to become healthy. You can practise right attitudes. You can contact a healer. You can plug yourself into the life force.

And if you want to know more about the enormous power that can make you well, keep you healthy and solve all your problems, you have only to ask.

Chapter 5

HOW TO BE A SUCCESS

AFTER you have read the first four chapters of this book, put it down for a while and practise what I have recommended. In a remarkably short time you should be feeling much better. Perhaps the best plan would be to read the book right through, and then to go back to the first four chapters and practise the techniques of achieving good health. But whatever method you use be assured that you will soon start to feel fine.

When you do you will want to use your newly-found strength and good health. That is what it is for. Use some of it to make yourself a success. We all want to be successful. This is a natural and even laudable feeling.

As you know by now I do not give much thought to the past. It is over and done with. Remorse, self-pity, continued anger or hate are not only unprofitable, they are corroding. But look back for a short while on your life. The only use we can make of the past is to learn from it. This is where I want you to learn from yours.

I have listed some phrases. Read each one. Ask yourself if you have ever used these or something like them.

Nothing ever turns out right for me, what is the use of trying?

Failure and bad luck seem to follow me around.

I'm just unlucky and accident prone.

I've been let down so often I'll never trust anyone again.

Nothing I touch succeeds. I seem destined for failure.

I'm self-conscious. I do not get on with people.

I am a bad mixer. There is nothing I can do about it.

I would have been a success if I had not lost my leg, arm, hearing, loved one, dog, home (strike out which is not applicable).

Be completely honest with yourself. Read through the list again. Go into a room on your own and read the list aloud. Put a pencil mark against the lines that apply to you, for these are the excuses that most failures use. These are the alibis for lack of success.

Like most excuses they are not based on fact. They are merely a reflection of a state of mind.

Your state of mind is reflected in your attitude. You know now that your attitude can make you ill. It can also make and keep you well. Your attitude can do other things for you. It can control events. It can influence the people you meet.

As with healing you can use two sources of power. The first is the untapped power within you. The second is the help you can plug into from outside. I intend to show you how to use both of these. Let us have a simple example of how an attitude works for you.

Take two men, in their middle thirties, married with two children. They are professional men newly set up in practice. And they have overdrafts at the bank. The bank manager writes to each one. He says the overdraft is too high and wants it reduced. He asks each to call on him.

The first to be shown into the bank manager's office is nervous. He is good at his job, but has little confidence in the future. He sits there fidgeting, not looking the manager in the face, apologising and worried.

Maybe he has a good practice, some useful clients and connections. Within a few months the fees will start coming in and he will be able to reduce the overdraft. But his attitude is one of defeat. He is not surprised when the bank tells him it is calling in the loan.

The other man has a similar practice. He knows

that within six months he will be able to repay the bank. He has set out on paper all his assets and listed the professional work he has in hand. He goes through this with the manager. He tells him the plans he has for getting more work, expansion and widening his contacts. He even asks the manager to recommend the bank's clients to him. The bank does not foreclose on this one. In fact, he gets an extension of time.

The first man will use one of his alibis. He would have been all right if the bank had not foreclosed. He was just unlucky. Nothing ever works for him. He would have been all right if he had not lost his mother. Nothing ever turns out right for him. What is the use of trying, etc., etc.

The second man has found the secret of success. He does not use alibis or excuses. He looks facts in the face. He has discovered that his attitude can influence people. He is on his way to success. If you want to be successful you must follow the pattern that leads to success. You must become a doer. Instead of using excuses you must get up and go. The best antidote for failures is action. The best answer when things go wrong is to start putting them right.

Nobody at any time is completely defeated. You may have many setbacks. Get up. Dust yourself down. Analyse where you went wrong. With this extra protection start again.

I remember reading the story of one of the world's greatest insurance men. He started selling life insurance. You may think you have a difficult job. Try selling life insurance. It is probably the most wearing and discouraging occupation for a newcomer to attempt.

Our man tried hard enough. He worked long hours. He called on prospects time and time again. He would visit a man in the middle of the night if he thought he might buy insurance.

After some months the salesman was tired, worn, disillusioned and broke. He sat in an hotel room and decided to throw in the towel. He knew a lot about life insurance. He had tried. He was a failure.

But this man was one who did not believe in excuses. He knew other insurance salesmen made good money, ran expensive cars, owned their own homes, lived well. What was wrong? He moved over to the dressing table and spread his papers out.

Then taking a notebook he wrote down the details of the few successful sales he had made. There were not many over the months. They had been just enough to stop him starving. Nevertheless, he knew that to some men he had been able to sell insurance. He thought that if he could analyse his very few successes, he might be able to apply the formula to the rest of his prospects.

The analysis did not take long. There seemed

to be only one common factor. Every man who had bought insurance had done so on his first or second visit. What had been tiring the salesman and limiting his efforts was the number of abortive calls he was making.

He worked hard. He worked long hours. And there in front of him was the reason. His frustrations nearly all came from the third, fourth, fifth and sometimes sixth calls he was making on the same prospect. Yet he had never sold a policy except on his first or second call!

He felt excited and elated. He went to bed resolved to put the results of his analysis into practice. From that moment he never called on any prospective buyer more than twice. If he had not made a sale by the second call he struck the man off his list.

It paid off. He could call on so many more people. He became more positive in his attitude. He started to sell insurance well. In time he outsold every other representative of his company. Today he is the president of one of the great insurance companies.

There is a moral in this story, which is a true one. Analyse your mistakes when they happen. Find out what went wrong. Put it right. Do not accept your excuses. Do not alibi yourself. If things are not going right, find out why and *do* something.

It is not enough to find out why and do nothing. That is what most of the failures do. They know they have made a mess of things. They may even be honest enough to see where the mistake lies. But they accept it. They assume wrongly that there is nothing they can do. There is. Do something. Never mind if you are a little unsure of the outcome. Get up and go.

Action is one of the greatest antidotes for failure. However negative the conditions that surround you seem, maintain a positive attitude. If you are being worried by a man to whom you owe money, go and see him. Maintain a positive, optimistic frame of mind. Keep an attitude of health, happiness and success. Remember, as with health, the attitude works even if it is simulated initially. You will find it works for you.

There is no such thing as luck. You make your luck. You had better read that again. It is the key to success. YOU MAKE YOUR LUCK.

How often have you heard somebody say: " Oh, he was lucky. He just happened to be in the right spot at the right time." This is the excuse of the failure. The speaker is saying he was unlucky because he was not in the right place at the right time. The other man's success is just good luck. His failure is bad luck. Other people's luck is used as an excuse for your failure.

The truth is more likely to be that a man concentrated his entire waking life on a particular project. If he was an insurance salesman, for instance, he ate, drank, thought and acted insurance all the time. He became saturated in the world of insurance and the selling of it. Whenever he was having a drink, meeting someone in his club, taking lunch or riding in a train, he talked and thought insurance selling.

As a result, he was attuned to the finest ripple on the surface of the sea of opportunity. When that ripple came in the form of a mere hint that a big policy could be sold to a certain prospect, he was off like a flash.

Because he was there first, he was good at his job and adopted a positive and helpful attitude, he sold the insurance. Afterwards, the ones who did not said he just happened to be there at the right time. This is their excuse for not being there.

If you are going to stop being a failure and start being a success, do it now! Right now. Let this simple truth stand before you.

DESIRE BRINGS SUCCESS.
FEAR ATTRACTS FAILURE.

Since we are going to cast out all negative thoughts, let us abandon the last statement. What we have left is the simple truth. *Desire brings success*. This means what it says. If you want something you will get it. You will have to want it very much. You will have to keep your desire in front of you at all times. The desire must have a good motive. It will not work if your desire is to corrupt or do evil. But if your motive is to be successful in a moral field then be assured it will work out.

When you want something enough you just have to do something about it. There are two ways to get to the top of the tree. One is to find an acorn, sit on it, and wish. The other is to start climbing upwards. This is what you must do. When I used the word " desire," I did so purposely. Because desire is what you need. Wishful thinking and dreaming may pass the time pleasantly enough. They will achieve nothing. What achieves results is desire, translated into action.

Let us sum up where we are so far. You are going to find out your alibis and discard them. You are going to forget the past events and remember only the lessons you learned. You are going to analyse your failures and find out where you went wrong. You are going to decide the success you want and to DESIRE it strongly enough to do something about it. Fine. Where do we go from here?

We must now start influencing both events and people. There is a technique for this. From now you are not going to sit back and let events take their course. You are going to make events happen. Yes, you can do this. Here is how.

When I wrote that desire brings success, I could have expanded this sentence. But I wanted to keep it short so that you would remember it. If I had written it in full, I would have said, " Desire brings success through opportunity linked with action."

You now know what you want to achieve. Keep your goal an immediate one. If you are a salesman, for instance, do not aim at this moment at being the chairman of the board of directors. You may well be in time. But you need a short-term target. Your target will be to be the most successful salesman in your area.

Keep that simple target in mind. Think about it. Make it your immediate desire. Say it to yourself each morning, " I am going to be the most successful salesman in my area." Then get to know your product really well.

The essence of salesmanship is selling yourself. But you must know your product well enough, and have sufficient faith in it, to be able to sell yourself with a clear and honest mind.

You start the day with two advantages. The first is that you have a simple goal. You are going to be the most successful salesman. The second is that you know your product well. Adopt an attitude that reflects both these facts. You are alert, optimistic, positive. Then when you see your first prospective customer, DO NOT TRY TO SELL HIM ANYTHING.

No, it is not a printing error. Do not try and sell. Your initial needs are first to find something interesting in the person you are meeting. The second is to render a service to him. People are basically the same. If you flatter them by being interested in them, they will respond.

Start talking. Find out what his interests are. Show an interest in them yourself. Then wait an opportunity to do something for him. Render him a service. The essence of all sound relationships is reciprocation.

If you show that you are interested in a man, he gets interested in you. If you render somebody a service he feels he should do something for you. The thought processes may be subconscious and not obvious, but they are there. The service you render may be small. It does not matter. Find what you can do for him and do it. This always works. You will then make your first sell.

I have taken the example of a salesman because it is an easy one to demonstrate. But what I have written applies to us all. We will get much more out of people if we put much more in.

Showing an interest in what the next man is doing stimulates his interest in you. He feels good. When he feels good his body starts getting into balance. He begins to feel well and happy because your attitude has influenced his attitude.

Attitudes are amazingly infectious. It is difficult, for instance, to keep a straight face when you are in a room full of laughing people. It is not easy to be happy at a funeral. Attitudes infect the people in contact with them. Your attitude will change the men and women you meet. If you are happy, well, optimistic and interested in your fellows, they, too, will feel better and become interested in you.

When you render a service, however small, the reaction is gratitude. It may not be expressed immediately, because there may not be the opportunity. But as you maintain these attitudes with everybody you contact, you will soon have dozens of people who wish to create opportunities for reciprocation. Then one day, and soon, one of these men or women will create an opportunity for you. You will be able to take a big step upwards in the ladder of success.

How are you going to apply this to your entire life? It does call for a complete change in attitudes. You will need to think and act differently. Start by defining your short-term goal. Look upwards to the next step in the ladder. Make that your goal. Do not look to the top. Look up one step only.

Every morning think about the step you want to make. Get it well into your head and keep it there. You will not alter your target until you have hit it dead centre. Then you will shift your aim to the next target up the line. But not until then.

Start your day with your first goal in mind—well in mind. But you need to do nothing directly to achieve it. Your next direct action must be to contact as many people as you can conveniently do during your working day. I use the word " contact " because you may do it by personal call or by telephone. The personal call is best.

Talk to and meet as many people each day as you can. Needless to say, they should be people connected with your goal. If you are in business then make them business people. Do not go out of your way to meet strangers who may be unconnected with your normal day. Meet, instead, those whom you should meet because they are part of the business world you inhabit. And meet as many as you can.

You are now increasing the odds enormously on success. You are meeting people, dozens of them, every day. And they are people connected with your immediate goal. But do not discuss that goal. And do not seek to achieve it. Not now. You have put yourself in a contrived position. In your mind is firmly fixed the immediate goal you

wish to attain. It is there engraved on your mind
and on your subconscious. This is how it will
work for you.

With everybody you meet today seek an
opportunity to serve them. Your service can be
a small one that takes very little effort, or a big
one than means putting yourself out. The size and
the inconvenience to you of the service you render
is of no moment. What matters is that to each
person you meet today you render a service, however trivial. This is all you have to do.

You may end this day without having achieved
your goal. Be patient. You have sown many seeds.
Give them time to sprout. Tomorrow you are going
to sow a lot more. And the next day, and the
next.

Every day, you are going out of your way to
meet as many people as you can. To each you
will render a service. Every week there will be
dozens of people who are itching to respond. Be
assured that some of them will find a way to do
so. When they do you are waiting. You have no
rehearsed favour to ask them. You wish no special
service. But remember that your immediate goal
is firmly engraved on your conscious and your
subconscious minds.

You will be pleasantly surprised at the number
of opportunities you will be given to achieve it.
When you have hit your first target, abandon it.

Set your sights at the next target up the line. Fix it firmly in your mind to replace the one you have already hit. And start again the same successful formula.

Meet as many people as you can. Render them a service. And keep on doing this. You will start hitting those targets sooner and sooner. And since success breeds success, people will soon start to seek you out. You will be on your way to your ultimate goal.

When you have achieved it, people will look at your success and immediately alibi their own lack of it. "He was lucky," they will say, "he just happened to be at the right place at the right time." But you and I . . . we know better.

Chapter 6

HOW TO ATTRACT MONEY

MOST people want to be rich. Some are content with their lot, but most of us feel that life would be easier if we had more in the bank. Let me assume you are one of these. If you are not, then skip this chapter. It is not for you. You are one of those fortunate people who have tailored their needs to their earning power.

You live carefully within your income and do not aspire to have more material possessions or greater luxury than you now enjoy. Good for you. You have reached maturity and do not need this chapter. You may not even need this book.

The majority of people I meet want to have more than they have. Sometimes the desire is reasonable, like the nurse who felt many of her troubles would go if only she had the money to buy a small car. Or like the lonely old-age pensioner who felt he would be less lonely if he had a television set.

These may seem modest requirements. They are vastly different from the business man running a three-car family who wants a yacht, or the woman who yearns for a diamond necklace. But they all have the same basic need. They want more money.

This chapter is headed, " How to attract money." The word " attract " was chosen purposely. I could have called it, " How to make money." But that is not what you are going to learn. Very few people make money. Counterfeiters make a good copy of it at times. But the price is too high for most of us, and in any case it is illegal.

The mint makes money legally. But few of us can get a job there. It must be frustrating at the end of the week to be allowed to take so little of it home.

If you found oil on your land you might consider you were making money. They do call it " black gold." If you found gold or buried treasure you might imagine you were making money. But generally you cannot make money. All you can do is to attract to yourself as much or more than you need.

Let us assume the amount of money is fairly constant. Imagine you are living on an island. Through this land flows a fresh water stream. It comes from an opening in the mountains. It flows down towards the sea. The flow of water is constant. It is the only source of fresh water.

To live you have to raise crops. To do this you need to irrigate your land. You therefore build a dam and divert just enough water to fill your carefully-dug irrigation trenches. The rest you let flow for the benefit of your neighbours.

Some men are lazy. They do not dig proper canals. They do not even make a good dam. Their land is poorly irrigated. The crop is inadequate for their needs. Other men are industrious. Their land is well irrigated and their crops are good.

Some men are greedy. They build dams that are much bigger than they need. Their irrigation canals are full. They divert the surplus water into tanks. They can then afford to employ their less industrious neighbours to till their land. They can sell any surplus water.

In time they can buy the land adjoining and use their surplus water to make it give good crops. The ex-landowners now become their labourers. Eventually a few men own most of the island. They are the rich ones. The labourers are the poor. The few industrious men who have maintained their independence form the middle class.

Money is like this water. It is flowing around you. You cannot create it any more than you can make it rain. All you can do is to attract it to you. When you have more than you need, you are rich. When you have too little you are poor. Before we start to examine the technique of attracting money let us look at why you want it.

It is difficult not to spend money today. Advertising has reached a high peak of efficiency. All our waking hours we are assailed by clever inducements to spend. In the morning you pick up your newspaper to find it full of advertisements encouraging you to spend. Buy a magazine and the full-page coloured advertisements are often better done and more attractive than the editorial matter.

Look out of the window and the hoardings scream at you. Walk down the street and shop windows lure you to look and buy. Go home and watch television and the screen coerces you to spend your money.

Everything is better, cheaper, cleaner, easier, shinier and pinker than the things you already have. Buy. Buy. 3p off. Bigger. Better. Cheaper. Gimme . . . Gimme . . . Gimme.

And if you do not have any money, no matter. You can have credit. Buy it now. Pay later. Only one pound down and the balance over two years. Use your credit card. Charge it to your account. Have a credit sale. Take out a hire purchase agreement. Have it NOW. Pay later.

It is becoming impossible to resist the demands made on our purses by advertisers who have made the extraction of their contents a science. Advertising and merchandising techniques are designed to make you feel that what you have is obsolete, what you lack to make you happy can be acquired, and that a full life, happiness, sexual opportunity and satisfaction depend on the purchase of what they are selling.

It is not surprising that we feel frustrated when we do not have enough money to satisfy these needs, even if we have a suspicion that the needs are over-stimulated.

We live today in a materialistic society. To many of us our success is measured by precise status symbols. The type of car we drive is one. The size and location of the house we own is another. The clothes we and our wives wear, the places we go to on holiday, and how often we do get away, the schools our children attend, the interior furnishing of our homes, the state and size of the garden, the ownership of a swimming pool, a yacht, a villa on the Mediterranean, a title and a Savile Row tailor—these are a few of the status symbols.

Add to these money in the bank, unused assets, and the ability to spend without bothering to count the pennies, and your neighbours are not the only ones who think you are rich. You do, too.

I do not condemn the wish to attract money. In the environment in which twentieth-century urban man exists this desire is understandable. But I hope you will be sufficiently mature to limit your desires. It is the only way you can get any happiness from the pursuit of material riches. If you limit your desires you will not escalate your acquisitiveness.

When you have a car, perhaps it is enough. Then your wife wants one of her own. Soon you need not a means of transport but a status symbol. The car becomes a Rolls Royce. Your wife will not be seen driving the sort of car her less prosperous neighbours have. She needs a foreign sports car. Your neighbours holiday in Majorca, you have to go to Jamaica. Your friend next door has a twenty-one inch television set, you have to have one with colour. So it goes on.

Eventually your desires for immediate material possessions are sated. Then you start accumulating money for the sake of doing so. You become a millionaire. Then one million is not enough. You need two millions, three or more.

I feel pity for millionaires. I regard them in the same light as I do drug-takers. The millionaire is addicted. He cannot possibly need the money he diverts into his pockets. Yet he goes on flogging ceaselessly a successful formula because it diverts more and more of the money to him and out of circulation. Poor man!

Mind you, there is no great merit in poverty. Poverty is a state of mind. I do not regard it as any test. It is rather a condemnation of a man's inability to use the gifts bestowed on him. The real test is riches.

Money is power. With money you can feed the starving, clothe the naked, house the homeless, educate the ignorant and bring warmth, understanding, comfort and compassion to those in need. When you have attracted more money than you personally need then you have the power to do all these things.

Remember that you are here as part of your spiritual education. It is what you do with what you have that counts. With money you have the power to do good. It is interesting to see what rich men do with their money. Most of them try to found some form of dynasty. They go in for complex financial manoeuvres so as to avoid death duty. They set up trusts, arrange to get as much as they can out of the country, go to enormous lengths to see that their family is able to continue to live at the same standard of luxury after they are dead. I cannot think why.

There is a universal fallacy held by most parents. They want to see their children carry on where they leave off. This just is not possible. Each of us has reached a different stage of our spiritual evolution. Your child may be more advanced than you. To him your money and its accumulation may seem a lifetime wasted. Another may be at an early stage of spiritual evolution. To give such a child the enormous power that great wealth confers is like handing a loaded gun to an idiot.

Great wealth brings the greatest responsibility. I know of no millionaire who has measured up to this test. The acquisition of money is in itself a pursuit that destroys moral values. By the time you have made it you are unqualified to use it.

But let us assume you do not want to be a millionaire. Good for you. You are limiting your desires. This is maturity. You just want enough to live a little better. All right. I will now introduce you to the method of attracting money. But a word of warning. This is like lighting a fuse. You are going to initiate something you may be unable to stop. The explosion may destroy you. Because unless you continue to limit your desires you will keep applying the formula until you destroy any ability to use it for good. So before we touch the match to the fuse let us take a few precautions.

Let us examine our motives. Why? Why do you want money? I want you to put this book down. Take a piece of paper and a pencil. Jot down the motives you have for wanting money. Do not list all the things you want to buy. List the motives. I am not going to help you in this. I do not know you well enough. You are on your own. At the end of this paragraph is a row of stars. They help to find your place to start reading again. Now write down your motives for wanting more money. Do it now.

*   *   *

Done it? Good. I hope you were honest with yourself. I cannot tell. You can. Were you? Were you honest? I am sure you were. Now look at what you have written and apply one simple test. Is your motive a good one? Is it moral, has it a good aim, does it contribute to the health, happiness and well-being of somebody other than yourself?

If your motive is good, the method of attracting money you are now going to learn will work. If your motive is wrong, evil, corrupt, or completely selfish then it will not work for you. I am sure it was none of these things. Your motives are fine. So let us read on.

You are now almost ready to start. But before doing so you need to limber up. Any athlete, however fit, will undertake limbering up exercises before he attempts the course. You must do the same. The first exercise is to rid your mind of guilt, yes, guilt.

We have been conditioned for years to accept that there is something fine in poverty and corrupt in riches. As a child you were told stories about the poor but good tenants and the rich but bad landlord. The worker was good. The boss was bad.

Riches were invariably associated with corruption and poverty with purity.

We use the phrase "filthy lucre" because making money has been regarded as a dirty thing. And people look down on the man who does some task purely for the money. This is all nonsense. There is nothing wrong with attracting money provided your motives are sound and your methods moral. So let us get rid of any ideas you might have of guilt towards money.

It is my earnest belief that we were not intended to be ill. We are designed to enjoy full and robust good health. Most sickness is man-made. I believe, too, that we were intended to enjoy riches, comfort and a full life. Like sickness, poverty is manmade. So get rid of those childhood inhibitions. You want to attract money. Good for you.

There is one more limbering-up exercise you must do. This is to discard any idea that you were not destined to have money. Poverty is a state of mind. Those who are poor, and have not the courage or the knowledge to alter their lot, have learned to use their condition as an alibi. They say they were not meant to have riches. They were destined to be poor. Rubbish! What they are disclosing by this attitude is their philosophical bankruptcy. Have nothing to do with this line of thought. You are not destined to be poor. You can attract money.

I will show you how.

So now you have done your two limbering-up exercises. You have got rid of any feeling of guilt about having money. You have refused to accept that poverty is your natural lot. Never again let these two thoughts intrude into your mind.

Let us start attracting money by having a modest target. Do not try to become very rich right away. It takes time and dedication. And along the way you may find it not as attractive a condition as you imagined. Make your immediate goal a more modest one. You must decide it. You know how much money you need at the moment, and how much will tip the balance, from want to comparative luxury. You can start with an immediate goal of attracting £100 or £1,000 or any other sum. It is up to you. But fix a sum and write it down. Use a felt-tipped pen and a postcard. Write on it in solid block letters, I AM GOING TO ATTRACT £1,000 TO ME. But, of course, for the £1,000 substitute any figure you like.

Keep the card in your pocket. When you have a moment take it out and read it. Read it aloud first thing in the morning and the last at night. Your immediate goal will thus become engraved on your subconscious mind. You are already on your way to attracting that sum of money. You have cleared your mind of guilt and of any inferiority complex. You have decided upon your immediate goal, and you have imprinted it upon your mind.

Now I want you to envisage your receiving that £1,000. It does not matter what mental picture you choose. For instance, you could be sitting in the office of your bank manager. He is shaking your hand and saying to you, "Congratulations, your account is £1,000 in credit." Or you could picture yourself sitting in your home with £1,000 in £5 notes piled up on the table. You are counting them. You turn to your wife and say, " Darling, we have £1,000."

It does not matter on what picture you decide. But it must be a positive and simple one. And once you have fixed it in your mind you must not change it until you alter your target. This system of picturisation is a proven method of gearing your efforts to one goal. It works.

Now when you read from your card the words, I AM GOING TO ATTRACT £1,000 TO ME, your mind will automatically turn on the picture you have chosen. The words will be synchronised with the picture. As you read the words you will see the picture of yourself receiving the money. These words and this picture must become something that you experience many times a day. When you are in the train, in a bus, driving a car or sitting at your desk, you will find time to say the words and to visualise the picture.

Your next step is to meet as many people as you can. Cut down on your letters and telephone calls. In your business, and in your social life, make as many personal contacts as you can. You need these contacts. The people you meet do not have to be rich and influential. The girl who is a typist and not very well off may lead you to the tycoon for whom she works. The elderly and somewhat vague old gentleman may have connections that you could not know about.

In any case you must not seek out people whom you think can help you. You must just aim at increasing your daily contact with people. On no account try and promote yourself. Indeed, the very opposite will bring the results you need.

Try instead to render a service to each one. The service can be as trivial as finding a stamp for a woman who wants to post a letter urgently, or getting a taxi for an old man who is not as agile as he used to be. It can be as simple as finding and writing down the name and address of a good garage, or taking your coat off and helping a man to change a wheel.

You will soon find that something wonderful is happening. In next to no time you will have your £1,000. Then you set on your next target, decide on your new picturisation (and it must be an absolutely new one) and you are ready for your next £1,000 or £5,000 or whatever.

Now you may not believe that a system as simple as this works. I assure you it does. Please try it. It cannot do you any harm. And think of what you will do with the money.

It works when you honestly apply all the essentials. Let us go over them:

1 Clear your mind of any feeling of guilt or inadequacy.
2 Make certain that your motives are good.
3 Fix an immediate monetary goal and write it down.
4 Decide on a simple picturisation of your attaining that goal.
5 Repeat the words of your goal and visualise your attaining it every morning, every night, and several times a day.
6 Increase as much as you can your contacts with people.
7 To everybody you meet try to render a service however small.

What you have succeeded in doing by this simple method is what every successful man does. You have cleared your mind and then firmly orientated it towards attaining a specific goal. You have then increased the opportunities of attaining that goal. You have made a good impression on everybody you have met. You have thrown your bread upon the waters. Soon the cake will come pouring in, £1,000 of it.

Chapter 7

THE KEY TO WEALTH

YOU may think that having just read a chapter headed, " How To Attract Money," this one is not necessary. But it is. Because money and wealth are not words that can be interchanged. We have come to think of money and wealth as having the same meaning. They do not. Money is a medium of exchange, a method of measuring the value of assets. Many assets cannot be valued. How do you value good health, for instance? How much do you think a crippled millionaire confined to a wheelchair for life would give for the ability to walk? What is the price of happiness?

Many people have tried to define wealth. The definition I like best is, " Having an abundance of what is desirable." I like this because it is so flexible. To a wandering Arab in the desert water is probably the most desirable commodity. If you told him that he could have in his tent a small metal object that, when he turned it in his hand, gave an unending supply of fresh, clean, cold water, he would think you were promising him the proverbial magic lamp.

But *you* have such a device. It is called a tap. You may think that a trunk full of money would make you wealthy. It may at the moment represent wealth to you. What good would it do if you were ship-wrecked on an uninhabited island with no food? You would gladly trade in the whole trunkful for a case of canned food.

Imagine that you are away one night and thieves break into your house. There is nothing of great value there except an oil painting. You had taken your entire capital and invested it in an old master. You cannot afford the heavy insurance, so it is uninsured. That is what the thieves take. You never get it back. Your entire capital is lost.

But suppose that you are a doctor. On your wall is your certificate which you received when you graduated. You have invested your entire capital in your medical education. The thieves take the certificate. It represents years of work and a great deal of money. It, too, is not insured. Would you worry? No, of course not.

Your wealth is in your mind, in your hands, in your experience, in the goodwill you have built in your profession. You can soon get a duplicate certificate. But why bother? The riches of the mind cannot be stolen.

Now, perhaps, you are beginning to see what

this chapter is all about. It is about having an abundance of what is desirable. Desirable to whom? Desirable to you, of course. Which brings us to the important question. What do you want? I cannot tell you. You have to decide this for yourself.

Perhaps you think money is all you need. I know a few men who have a lot of money. They do not seem to be happier or better than those who have less. A man who has made his first £10,000 will probably be trapped into trying to make £25,000. Then his goal becomes £50,000 or £100,000. Eventually he may become a millionaire. He meets others who have similar riches. If he can make a million, why not two, or three, or four? It is an addiction. The discovery that they have successfully operated a formula to divert more money to themselves than they can ever need seems always to bring with it the desire to see how far it can be pushed. The end is lost (if it was ever properly defined) in the fascination of the means.

This sort of avarice requires a certain type of dedication. As Emerson so wisely said, " A man is what he thinks all day." The self-made millionaire may present a façade of maturity, but under the thin veneer is a deep insecurity. He probably suffers from an inferiority complex, an unhappy home life and a fixation about his inadequacy in certain spheres. Never, ever, envy the wealthy. You cannot know the price that has been paid. There is an old Spanish proverb, " Take what you want, said God, take it and pay for it."

So what do you want under the heading of wealth? Stop reading. Get that piece of paper and a pencil again. Write down what you find desirable. Head it " Wealth," and underneath that write, " What I find desirable." Then list them. Go on. Do it now. Put this book down and do it. There is another row of stars so that you can find your place again easily.

*   *   *

Now you know. Read through the list and apply one single criterion to each thing you have written. Is it right? If you desire something that is wrong, immoral, corrupting or evil, you will not get it with my help. Now I know that we live in an age of excuses. Whenever somebody behaves badly there are many who rush to find an excuse. It was not really his fault. He was the victim of circumstances, environment, or heredity. And if the excuses are not available, then there are those who will always try and reduce the wrong. They say that we are old-fashioned, we do not understand, morality is out of date, everybody does it anyway.

To these excuse addicts I say, "Rubbish." There is and there always has been a clearly defined good and evil. It is not my function to put a tag on your every action. But you know that murder is wrong. You know that unselfish love is right. Deep inside you is the knowledge of what is right and wrong. Later in this book, when I deal with "How To Be Wise," we will discuss this in depth.

For the moment apply a simple test. The test is, "What are my motives?" If your desires are not motivated by evil or a wish to corrupt, they will probably be sound ones. As I have told you, it is not wrong to want to be wealthy. The desire to lead a good life and a full one is natural and praiseworthy. This is not the time to argue the question of right and wrong, good and evil.

I assume that your list contains most of the things people want. Your desires may be to have certain possessions, or to have a surplus of money to enable you to buy them. The possessions may be a new car, a colour television set, a cottage in the country, a swimming pool or a yacht. The variations are only a matter of degree.

You may also desire to live a full, interesting life, to travel and see the world, to meet people (or one special person). You may want to have children, to be a success as a singer, an architect, or a doctor.

You may also desire to see your name in lights, to write a best-selling novel, or to ride the winner in the Grand National. You may desire an apartment in the South of France, a villa in Switzerland and a house in London, with the money to equip and run them luxuriously. You may desire a good second-hand Mini or a brand new Silver Shadow Rolls-Royce.

I have asked many people over the years to list the abundance they feel desirable to them. The lists are surprisingly similar. Most people desire:

Health
Happiness
To be loved
Money, surplus to their needs
Peace and tranquillity
Security.

Compare what I have written to your list. Is it so different? And if you had all the things on my list would it matter very much if you missed some on yours? Be honest.

So when we get down to essentials, what really matters is the wealth of the mind. This, like the doctor's certificate, cannot be stolen from you. I have already shown you how to be healthy and how to attract money. Let us now together see how we can assure that we get and keep the wealth that matters. The wealth we are going to seek is buried under a lot of inhibitions. But it is there. When we dig together we will come to a strong box. When we open it we will find inside the treasure of:

PEACE HAPPINESS TRANQUILLITY SECURITY LOVE

Douglas Jerrold once wrote, " Happiness grows at our own firesides and is not to be picked in strangers' gardens." If you are not happy do not seek to excuse yourself. Do you have an alibi for your lack of happiness? Do you say, " I could be happy if I had a new car, lived in Tahiti, had a thousand pounds, was a millionaire, had a hi-fi set, lived in Capri, had a new camera, was married to Raquel Welch, had a cottage in the country, had a new suit, lived in the Bahamas . . ."?

Please cross out what is not applicable, or substitute your special excuse. But happiness has very little to do with possessions or environment. Happiness is simply a state of mind. Once you have learned the secret of inducing it you will be happy wherever you are and whatever you might own or lack. If you have not mastered the secret then you will be unhappy even if you are a millionaire and surrounded with possessions. This is a truth that has been appreciated for a long time. Pope, in his " Essay on Man," summed it up:

> " Condition, circumstance is not the thing,
> Bliss is the same in subject or in king."

The key to wealth is in your mind. That some people are successful and wealthy whilst others remain unsuccessful and poor is seldom due to any extraordinary skill. There are men with gifts, to be sure. The painter, sculptor, composer and musician all have gifts they have developed. But they are the exceptions. That is why their work is valued so highly.

The majority of people do not have these valuable gifts. The difference between the man who is wealthy and the one who is poor is his attitude. Because you are reading this chapter, I assume you are not wealthy.

If you are then you probably do not need this chapter. Good for you. But because you are reading it, I will assume that either you are poor or not as wealthy as you would like to be. Now, if you were embarking on any commercial venture, the first thing you would do would be to list your assets. So pick up that pencil again. Get a new sheet of paper and here and now let us together list your assets. Please do not try and do it in your head. You must write it all down.

You can start off by writing the word, " Freedom." Write that you live in the freest country in the world. You have freedom of beliefs, worship and action. There is no country anywhere with the same tolerance for the rights of the individual. Write that you have a roof over your head, warm and sufficient clothing, and enough to eat. There are many millions of people in the world today to whom freedom, good food, warm clothing and the comfort and privacy of their home represent undreamed of luxuries.

There are refugees in camps today who have been born and brought up in these transient and inadequate surroundings. They have never known a home other than a tent or a hut. They have never had any privacy. Their eating, washing, social intercourse and even defecating have to take place in communal surroundings.

There are millions of men, women and children who have never known what it is to have a full stomach. And they have not known this simple luxury for two or three generations. In India there are old men who will die without ever during their lifetime once knowing the comfort of a bed and a square meal. They and their families have spent their entire lives sleeping in the gutters of a big city and living on scraps. Count your blessings, my friend.

Keep writing. Add that you are educated, sane, undeformed, able to work and earn a good living.

You are healthy, articulate, capable of loving and being loved. Keep writing. You are going to need a few more sheets of paper. Count all your blessings. Do not omit the ones you take for granted.

You have a pair of reliable eyes; some are blind. You have two sensitive ears; remember the deaf. You have two legs. You can walk and run and jump; others are crippled. You have two arms; there are babies born with none.

You have been educated to a level that in the undeveloped countries would make you a seer amongst men. You can read and write. There are many millions of people who are still illiterate. Count all your blessings. And as you do so consider those who lack them.

By now you should have covered more than one sheet of paper. If you have been honest and conscientious your blessings will make quite a list. These are your assets. There are a lot more there than you thought you had, I will be bound. You are starting on the road to acquire wealth with a lot in your favour. In fact with a list of assets such as you have I do not see how you can fail. But just in case you feel that failure is still possible, let us take a long, cool look at failure.

One of the main things that makes the successful man different from his fellows is his attitude to failure. I have seen this operating so often that it now astounds me that others cannot always recognise it. The wealthy man must have made a lot of mistakes in his time. If you think that his wealth came easily and without effort then you will be wrong. Most successful men have gone through a long apprenticeship before reaching their present goals. A man who never made a mistake never made anything. But when one of these men made a mistake he bounced back and then went off at a different angle.

Suppose you are driving your car. You come to a roundabout. From it are radiating a great number of roads. You decide the one you want to take and drive down it. It starts to get foggy and visibility is down to a few yards. The surface of the road deteriorates and is eventually no more than a cart track. You battle on, peering through the side window, coughing away the fog, your eyes smarting, straining with the effort of keeping the car on the almost invisible track. After many miles of this you are lost. Then your lights faintly pick up something ahead. You press on only to find yourself up against a brick wall that completely blocks the track. You took the wrong turning. All your efforts have brought you to a dead end. What do you do?

This is where the difference between the two attitudes can clearly be seen. You rest for a while, then you get out of your car and explore the wall on either side of the track and across a field in an effort to find a way round the obstacle. You end up out of petrol, stuck in a quagmire, exhausted and thoroughly depressed. You decide you are a failure. You make up your mind to sell the car and walk in future. You may even convince yourself that you are not cut out to be a car owner, that you are the pedestrian type.

The other man looks at the blank wall ahead of him. His attitude is immediate. " This is not the way for me," he says. Without wasting any time or effort he turns the car round and heads back to the roundabout. He drives out of the fog, off the track onto a good road. At the roundabout he says that that road was obviously not the one for him. He tells himself he must find the one that is. He drives round the roundabout a few times. Then he makes his choice and goes careering enthusiastically along a new road. Maybe this one also ends against a brick wall. If it does he will try another. Failure to him does not exist. He is going to succeed. All he has to do is to find the right road.

This is the attitude you must adopt. A failure is no more than an indication that this is the wrong way, the wrong time or the wrong place for you. Discard it. Start looking for the right one. You must pick yourself up, dust yourself down, and try again. But do not try the same road. That is a cardinal mistake. Try another road. Your mind holds unlimited wealth. You must give it the opportunity to exploit it. Your list of assets showed that you had all the capital you need to succeed. What you must add to this great store of unused assets is energy.

It was Daniel Webster who said, "Failure is more frequently from want of energy than from want of capital."

The advantages of not succeeding sometimes is that it is the very best method of learning. Any fool can profit from his successes. You are not a fool. You are going to profit from your failures. If you know that that turning leads to a cart track which peters out to a dead end, then you will never take that turning again. You will look for different roads to your goal.

But there are men who do not do this. They will drive down the same road time and time again, hoping that somebody has made up the track or knocked down the wall that blocks it. And when they find the circumstances unchanged (the track is still as impassable as before, the fog obscuring the way, and the road ahead blocked by an impassable wall) they moan at their failures and resolve to have another go some other time. But they resolve to go down the SAME ROAD.

Now you can see the difference of attitude between the failure and the success, between the wealthy and the poor? It is a state of mind. The wealthy regard a blank wall as a clear and useful indication that they should try another road. The poor regard it as the end of their efforts and a sign that they are not meant to go ahead. By this time you must have realised that

THE KEY TO WEALTH IS THE RIGHT ATTITUDE.

Let me give you one more example. A man has built a large, successful business. He is wealthy by any standards. He earns a lot of money, has a lovely home with a swimming pool, runs three cars, is well dressed and lives to a high standard. His wife and his children are well turned out. She lives a life of ease; they go to first rate private schools. This man is healthy, wealthy and happy. By any standards he is a success.

Then there is a financial crisis. He suffers a severe loss. He comes home one evening and tells his wife that he has lost everything—his business, home, possessions, money. The deciding factor as to whether he regains and even improves on his previous position or accepts failure as a permanent condition is his attitude.

He may say: " I am beaten. I have lost everything. I will get a job and earn a few pounds a week, just enough to keep us all. The children will have to leave their schools. We must go and

live in a council house. I am a failure. Finished."
Then he will be finished indeed.

But suppose he says to his wife: " Darling, we
still have each other. We still have our love. We
still have fine children, our health, strength,
ability to laugh and enjoy ourselves. We still have
our spiritual maturity, the strength of its awareness, our friends and the many, many assets not
represented by purely material things. I still have
the same brain, the same memory, the same skills.
This is a mistake from which I have learned much.
I built a big and successful business before, when
I knew less and had much less experience. I can
do it again and I will." Of course he will.

I believe that most of us tap only about ten
per cent of our potential. Our minds have a
capacity that is largely untouched. We should
learn to extend ourselves and continually search
for more opportunities to do so. There is no such
thing as failure. It is merely an excuse, a state of
mind, an alibi for laziness, a lack of faith, a low
moral fibre.

When patients come to me with a long tale of
woe I often tell them to look for a moment at
Helen Keller. Soon after she was born she became
both stone deaf and completely blind. Can you
imagine what this means? It would be bad
enough if it happened to an adult. He would have
had an education. He could speak and communi-

cate. He would know what things looked like. He would have a vast fund of knowledge and understanding and experience to call upon.

But Helen Keller was a little baby when this happened to her. She could hear nothing, see nothing, receive no communication from anybody, make no contact with the people around her and the unknown world into which she was born. She was seemingly irrevocably cut off from learning, from communication, from experience. She grew up in a dark void, soundless, speechless, sightless.

Yet she dedicated her life to helping handicapped people. With all these potential alibis, this was the woman who spent her whole life helping those *less fortunate,* those who lacked the positive attitude she had. This was the woman who at the age of 75 journeyed from America to the Far East to aid handicapped men, women and children there. This was the woman who said, " Defeat is nothing to be ashamed of ; it is routine in digging the gold of one's personality."

Chapter 8

HOW TO LIVE A FULL LIFE

WOULD you like to live a full life? Of course you would. It sounds fine. But what do you mean by a full life? Would a continual programme of enjoyment constitute a full life? Emile Zola once wrote that he would like to start a new religion with one commandment only, " Enjoy thyself." If you had the money to travel, own a big car, have a villa on the Mediterranean, eat rich foods, drink champagne with every meal, be waited upon hand and foot and wear expensive clothes: is this living a full life? Or is it living a selfish and empty one?

I think you are capable of greater things. I think that you might have a lot of fun in this way, but after a surprisingly short while it would pall. You would feel empty and dissatisfied. You would want to do something more rewarding. That last word is the key, " rewarding," because a constant process of taking and not giving eventually produces an arid and futile life. Something is lacking.

We all like to enjoy the good things. We all like to have holidays in the sunshine, to go out sometimes for a memorable meal, to drive a fast and comfortable car, to have new clothes, to live a little more fully. But a constant diet of sugar is cloying to the palate. We need the more simple tastes so that we can appreciate the finer things when we are offered them.

John Stuart Mill wrote, " I have learned to seek my happiness by limiting my desires, rather than in attempting to satisfy them." Does this make sense to you? Or do you think the man was merely finding an excuse for his lack of ability to provide something better?

You must decide in your own way what constitutes a full life. Your criteria will change as you change. When I was younger I used to think that driving a Bentley and eating gastronomic masterpieces twice a day with a beautiful blonde was a full life. Today I have a Bentley, but I hardly ever use it. I do not eat meat and I seldom take a drink, so that my meals are simple and frugal. And as I am married to a tall, shapely blonde I can sit opposite her every day of the week.

But now I have a different standard. In ten years' time it will have altered and, I hope, matured still further. A full life is the product of your imagination. The man who loves the sea might dream of owning a small yacht. There are others who get seasick on Brighton Pier and who regard any sea voyage as purgatory. A mountaineer might consider a full life consisted of climbing higher and higher, but a man who had a fear of heights would not.

Whatever constitutes a full life, there can be no doubt that it will be easier to achieve if you are well. By this I do not mean that you are not ill. I mean that you have the positive attribute of robust, abounding good health, of body and of mind. We have been into this in the previous chapters. So let us assume that the full life starts with this condition.

You are fit, you are well, your mind is uncluttered by remorse for the past, or fear of the future. What else do you need? The next thing is bodily comfort. You should have a home of your own. I do not think it matters whether it is a castle or a cottage. Each has a different idea of what constitutes a home. One man will need a thatched cottage, a roaring wood fire and an acre of garden. Another is happier in a centrally heated town flat with the comfortable noise of traffic under his window. One may be happy at the top of a mountain, another prefers the sea shore. You may find the ideal home in a caravan, a yacht, or a tent. It is up to you. But a man needs a place to call " home." You alone can decide what fits your personal ideal.

Then you need to be warm and well clothed. Here, again, there can be no universal standard. The mountaineer's idea of clothing is far different from the man who lives on the shores of the Mediterranean. The town dweller may not feel at ease unless he is wearing a well-tailored suit. The farmer may be happier in a sweater and a warm windcheater.

It is the same with food. One man's ideal may be a daily plate of steak and chips. Another will require the *haute cuisine* of a *cordon bleu* chef. A third will be a vegetarian and consider a day empty without a salad dish. But all these are matters of personal taste.

Your taste is made up of the sum of your experiences to date. It will develop and change as you mature. The common denominator we can agree upon is that to live a full life you need to be healthy in mind and body, to have a home of your own where you can be comfortable and relaxed, to be well clothed and fed. What more do you need?

You need to have, or to be able to earn, enough money to maintain these requirements. And if you are married and have dependents, then you want to be able to maintain them in a like manner. You may feel that you need a number of purely material pieces of equipment to enable you to live as you wish. For instance, you may want a form of transport. One man will be content with a Mini, another will want a Rolls, one may like to ride a thoroughbred horse, another is happier on a bicycle.

If you enjoy music you may consider your life incomplete unless you have a piano, but a different musician would settle for a piccolo. Or you may appreciate music, but not be capable of making any and rely on a record collection and a hi-fi set.

You may be a prolific reader and need a library of books, or feel unfulfilled unless you are surrounded with paintings or works of art, or be most relaxed in front of your television screen. Different men want different things. But this is not living a full life. This is merely providing the environment you prefer.

There are two ingredients essential to the full life. Every great philosopher has reached the same conclusion. You may disguise them under different labels. You may decide that what I write is trite or banal. But the indisputable facts are that no man can live a full life without the magic ingredients of love and service.

I told you to believe nothing that cannot be proven to your personal satisfaction and to accept only that which makes sense. So far, you must admit, that what I have written makes sense. So go along with me a little further. I assure you that although this may seem like preaching it will continue to make sense.

The very survival of our civilisation may ultimately depend on the acceptance of this simple truth. Unless the brotherhood of man is recognised and acted upon, continued conflict between races, creeds and ideologies is inevitable. This world of ours is governed by natural laws. The brotherhood of man is one of the foundations of these laws. And " Love is the fulfilling of the law " (Romans xiii, 10).

If you are to live a full life then it is necessary to cultivate love for your fellows. This is sometimes not easy. You may find that you do not suffer fools gladly, that the ignorant and the selfish ones annoy you. This I understand. But it is essential for your good that you constantly seek to develop love and compassion for those around you. You do not have to agree with them, but you must try and understand them, and in disagreement feel kindly and sympathetic towards them.

Consider yourself as an electric generating station. You are well-designed, efficient, well-served and functioning as you should. In fact, your generators are humming in perfect balance, the turbines are spinning and the electricity is pouring along the wires. A generating station cannot store electricity. It has to adjust its production level constantly to meet the demands made upon it.

You are working well. But nobody is plugged into your grid, nobody has switched on. The demands made upon you are nil. There is nowhere for the power you are manufacturing to go. You have no alternative but to shut down the generators. You have to do it fast and you have to do it completely. Otherwise the plant will just blow up.

Well, you are a generating station. You are transmitting the power of the spirit. The current you use is not a.c. or d.c. or measured in volts, ohms or watts. The current your personal generating station uses is love. As long as it is being received and utilised by those that are in touch with you, then you are fine. You go on working as you should. But the moment it is no longer received you have to stop production.

Have you ever seen a big industrial complex shut down and abandoned? It is truly a sad sight, a great concept wasted. There is no greater concept than man. For him to work as he has been designed he needs to love those around him. If he stops, then the same type of decay sets in. Like a deserted and shut down factory his existence is without meaning.

From time to time I get into philosophical arguments with people. These I enjoy. It is a good thing to stretch one's mind as often as one can. I do not always agree with those I meet in this way, but I like hearing their views. When I have these discussions there is often a man who seeks to prove that there is no God, there is no design, that we are on this planet by chance and that life is purely a material thing that finishes absolutely when we die. He says that death is the end and seeks to convince me this is so.

I have listened to these arguments many times. If you assume the man is right, then you must eventually reach the conclusion that life is futile. Why make an effort when in the end everything dies and nothing survives? The only thing to do if you believe this philosophy is to have a wonderfully good time, to live so as to enjoy yourself without consideration for anybody else and to drown the feeling of utter futility that must eventually descend on you with wine, women, song and whatever amuses you more. But life is not futile. It has meaning.

Your life need not be futile. It can be fulfilling and meaningful. To make it so you must see that the power you generate is wanted and is used. You need to love and be loved. I am not writing of love in the meaning of passion or of sex. It is something much greater and more enduring than that. It is the love of humanity. It is the love that prompts you to adopt an attitude of compassion, sympathy and helpfulness towards everyone you come in daily contact with.

We all tend to be withdrawn at times. In the British this is a national characteristic. It is a bad one. In the close and complex society in which we live today every man is dependent on his neighbour. Happiness is founded on human relationships. Withdrawing into your own little world stunts these relationships or denies them. We become over concerned for our own problems.

Selfishness and egotism are the keys that open the doors to unhappiness and illness. Unselfishness and service to others open the way to contentment and the good health that comes with mental harmony. Your power station cannot function unless you can be assured that the current is being absorbed. The power you have available is love. The method of getting it distributed is service to others.

The old saying about casting your bread upon the waters is based on sound experience. When Arthur F. Sheldon was looking for the motto for Rotary International, he sought no further than this and produced, " He profits most who serves best."

This chapter is headed, " How To Live A Full Life." I know of no man who has achieved this end without the two essential ingredients of love and service. One without the other will not do the trick. Your power station will not function if it manufactures the power of love, but does not provide the method of distributing it through service. It will be just as frustrated if it organises the service, but lacks the power to make everything function.

I remember the tale of the woman who was interviewing a man for the job of butler. " Are you experienced in service?" She asked. " Yes, madam," he replied. " both kinds."

" What do you mean by both kinds?" she asked. " Well, madam," the man replied, " I can do the sort of service that makes them want to come again and the sort that makes them want to keep away."

I could fill this chapter with quotations to ram home the truth of what I write. Let me suffice with:

" Human brotherhood is not just a goal. It is a condition on which our way of life depends. The question for our time is not whether all men are brothers. That question has been answered by God who placed us on earth together. The question is whether we have the strength and the will to make the brotherhood of man the guiding principle of our daily lives."

John F. Kennedy

". . . the unity that binds us all together, that makes this earth a family, and all men brothers and the sons of God, is love."

Thomas Wolfe

" To be rich in admiration and free from envy; to rejoice greatly in the good of others; to love with such generosity of heart that your love is still a dear possession in absence or unkindness—these are the gifts of fortune which money cannot buy and without which money can buy nothing. He who has such a treasure of riches, being happy and valiant himself, in his own nature, will enjoy the universe as if it were his own estate: and help the man to whom he lends a hand to enjoy it with him."

Robert Louis Stevenson

" The vocation of every man and woman is to serve other people."

Count Leo Nikolayevitch Tolstoy

When the power station that is you continues to manufacture and to distribute the universal power of love all is well with you. The sun shines, you feel great, the problems that life presents are seen in their correct perspective and easily dealt with.

What happens when you do not? Imagine an

electrical generating station that was pushing out an a.c. current of 240 volts. Suddenly it changes. The electricity is no longer a.c. but is altered to d.c. The voltage is increased without warning from 240 to 450 volts. It would cause a lot of damage. Very quickly all the consumers would switch off. If they could find a way of sending the too powerful and unusable current coursing along the wires back to you they certainly would do so. This is exactly what happens to man.

The moment we stop sending out love and generate, say, hatred instead, we are sending out a force of the wrong type and power. The people who receive it can switch the sender off. That is why bitter and frustrated people are so very lonely. But man has the ability to send back the sentiments that he does not want to accept. The forces that hatred arouses are returned to the sender magnified many times. This is true of the other passions of envy, malice, anger, jealousy and scorn.

It is a rule that what comes back is stronger than what goes out. So when we allow these thoughts to emanate from us we are inviting them to be returned multiplied many times. The effect this has on personal happiness and on bodily and mental health has already been demonstrated. It can cripple. It can cause pain. It can kill. And it does all these things every day.

Selfishness is the fundamental basis of all un-happiness, sickness, crimes against humanity and society. The selfish man who cannot know or appreciate these simple truths is ignorant. It is the ignorant that are the source of all these ills. The man who believes that might is right, and that the strength of money, arms and force will be a safe shield, is a fool.

I cannot locate the origin of a quotation I have heard, " Violence is the last resort of the incompetent." But I like it better than " He who lives by the sword, shall perish by the sword." They are, of course, both right. When you start thinking in terms of power, force, violence and covetousness, you are sending out the wrong emanations. They will come bouncing back sooner than you think and will harm you.

What can you do when you meet these emanations? Remember the rule is that we get back whatever we give out, but that it is multiplied in the process. When you meet a man who is giving out the thoughts, actions and attitudes of anger, hatred, envy, covetousness or any other manifestations of his selfishness, you must look for and seek to bring out the good in him.

Do not tell me that with some people this is difficult. Nothing worth doing is ever easy. But since every man has a divine soul, since each body is the manifestation of an immortal spirit, the good there can be reached if you dig deep enough. People can be very wrapped up in their personal conceits, problems and delusions of superiority. It is your function to break through these wrappings. Hidden within is the pure gold of the spirit. It is such with every man.

The inability to find it is yours, not his. To start you must break the circle. He gives out the wrong thoughts. You can easily bounce them back to him multiplied. He, in turn, can repeat the process. It is, indeed, a vicious circle. Yet it can be broken quickly and efficiently.

You must stand firm and radiate only the power of love, compassion and understanding. You do not bounce back the bad thoughts. You let them fall to the ground and send out the all-powerful love, the greatest there is.

It is easy to say you cannot see any good in a certain man. Be assured it is there. Look deeper and you will find it. The search is worth while. You will also find there some of the treasures you need.

I remember an experiment tried in Germany under Hitler. He set up breeding farms for human beings. To these went the finest examples of young German men and women. They were examined for the characteristics that would produce " ideal " children. Only those possessing these qualities were allowed to breed.

The selection was based on physical and mental standards and were as thorough as medical and genetic science could make them. The men and women were, in fact, bred as thoroughbred animals are. And in due time they produced lusty infants. To the children, too, were brought all the scientific knowledge then available in the fields of nutrition, exercise, child care and diet. The babies were taken from their parents and were reared by experts in the finest environment science could devise.

The experiment was a failure. It had to be abandoned. Too many children grew up dull, listless and with a very low intelligence standard. Afterwards, when the system could be analysed by the Allied forces, it was found that throughout their conception, birth and rearing these children were consistently starved of one essential ingredient, love.

Try your own experiment. Go and buy two hyacinth bulbs. Pick two that are as near twins as you can get. Let them be in size, shape, colour and texture as alike as can be. Get two pots and bed them in one each, using the directions your garden shop gives you. Make sure that each receives exactly the same amount of soil, space, peat—of everything. You must end with two identical hyacinth bulbs, in identical bowls, with exactly the same content.

Put the two where they will thrive best. Whenever you move one, move the other to the same place. Give them both a measured amount of water whenever you water them. And if you add any supplement to the water see that each receives an identical amount.

If you carefully follow these instructions you should in time get two identical hyacinths. They should produce shoots at the same time, grow to the same height and flower and then fade at the same time.

But you are going to introduce an ingredient to the life of one bulb. That is love. See that each bowl can be identified. Make one blue, and one pink, if you like. When you water the blue bowl say nothing. When you water the pink bowl, talk to it. Tell it how much you love flowers in general and hyacinths in particular. Once every morning and evening, put your two hands around the pink bowl and give out to it the feeling of love.

" The man's mad," you say. " He's potty. He talks to hyacinths." No I am not. You must have heard the term " green fingers." What do you think this means? It means that a gardener who has green fingers loves his garden. He gives out love, understanding and comfort to his plants. He shows them care and compassion. He studies their needs, of course, but to his knowledge of horticulture he brings a love of plants, and they flourish as for nobody else. His garden is a mass of colour. His flowers are bigger and brighter and come up earlier and last longer than those of other gardeners.

We say he has green fingers. We mean that the plants under his care react to the power of his love for them.

Your hyacinth will, too. The blue one will provide the standard. The pink one will show its shoots first, grow to a greater height, bloom earlier and remain in flower longer than the unloved blue one.

I told you to believe nothing that could not be proved. I stick to that advice. This is a simple and inexpensive experiment. You do not have to accept that it works. Prove it, not to me, but to yourself.

Animals respond, too. In some areas animals are more sensitive than people. They will respond quickly to love. You must have seen this many times. There are horses that respond best to one particular groom, the dog that reacts to the slightest wish of his master.

All animals know the power of love. Next time you meet an animal try it for youself. Do not speak to it. But silently give out the thoughts of love and affection. Then wait for the reaction. It may be quicker and more delightful than you think.

What I have written in this chapter is not theory. It is based on the research done by philosophers and sages throughout time. It is tried and tested. It is a system that will work for you. If at this moment you are feeling unhappy, and if your life seems empty and not a little futile, then lay this book down and put this powerful medicine to work right away.

Get out of that comfortable chair. Go out and find somebody who needs help. It can be a lonely old man, a woman without visitors in hospital, somebody who is down on his luck, or a rich man made corrupt by the power his money brings. Or it may be somebody in your household to whom you have been less than kind lately.

To that person render a service. Whatever it is, do it with a good heart and with a smile. And then tell that person how much you admire him. Find something to praise, however hidden it might at first seem. Give to one man or woman love and service for a few moments, and in a remarkably short time the power of love will be returned to you.

One thing you must not do. Do not put this book down, snuggle deeper into your armchair, re-light your pipe, refill your glass and then pass judgement on what I have written. What you have read is not a theory about somebody else. It is a fact. And it is about you!

Chapter 9

THE KEY TO WISDOM

THERE is one mistake that everybody makes. We assume that wisdom is the prerogative of someone else. We go to a man, or to a book he has written, and there we seek infinite wisdom. We may get guidance. We may get knowledge. We may learn what others did in like circumstances. But we do not get wisdom.

You cannot get wisdom from another man. Wisdom is the quality of being wise, the ability to make personal use of knowledge, allied to spiritual perception. In order to achieve true wisdom we must receive spiritual guidance. This cannot come from or through another person. It is, in essence, a direct communication that comes from the source of life itself. In other words, you have only to ask. " Before they call I will answer, and while they are speaking, I will hear."

This is a serious book. It is based on personal experience. It is intended as a guide for modern people living in this complex and materialistic society. So far you have followed what I have written. But now, perhaps, you have read the first two paragraphs of this chapter, stopped and said, " Oh dear, he's gone all religious!"

I have not, I assure you. Think for a moment. Whatever your religious upbringing, were you not taught to do what the priest, or a book, told you? Were not your actions and your thoughts prescribed by somebody who, you were told, knew better? How many times have orthodox Christians been told to refer to the New Testament for the answer to all their problems, for a complete guide to living, for the wisdom that may light their years? How many orthodox Jews have referred to the Talmud for the answer to a problem of morality, ethics or business? How many Moslems have relied on the teachings of the Koran to see them through their day? How many Hindu have turned to Krishna? How many men have relied for their source of wisdom on the words of Confucius, Zoroaster or Mithras?

To whom do you turn when you feel deep within yourself the need of illuminating wisdom? You go to the teaching of a man, a prophet, a seer or a god. It is I who say differently. It is you who are the conventional and orthodox thinker. It is I who am the revolutionary.

Read on, my friend. And remember my two standards: believe nothing that does not make sense to you, and accept nothing that cannot be proven to you. The key words are " to you." You must be the judge of whether what I write is just " religion " or a great truth that was there all the time.

I am not suggesting that we ignore what has been written. What I want you to do is to keep these books, institutions or people in a correct perspective. They can do no more than offer suggestions as to how you should act and think. What you do is up to you. If you feel the need of guidance and illuminating wisdom to govern your life then you must seek it yourself.

The best advice I can commend to you is, " To thine own self be true." This means quite simply that you should be true to your own soul, for it is there that illumination will come. How do you do it? How do you make this voice speak, how do you hear, how do you know it is good advice, how do you know it will not lead you into trouble? Let me answer these questions.

In a previous chapter I told you how to plug into power. That is one way you can also open yourself to wisdom. When you are alone, relaxed and quiet, you state your problem and ask for the wisdom to deal with it properly.

Sometimes we have a problem that must be dealt with immediately. We do not have the time to go home, wait until evening and then have a quiet moment in the ideal environment. No matter.

Tune in wherever you are. Suppose you are at a business meeting. A big deal is going very wrong. The other men turn to you and ask you what to do. You do not know, yet you have to make a decision.

At that moment you can seek illumination. Sit down with a blank piece of paper and a pen. There and then list the pros and cons of the problem. Put down the gist of it all in the simplest terms. Then write who benefits and who stands to lose by taking the alternative ways outlined to you. Then write your motives.

At that moment sit back, close your eyes for a few moments and ask for help in making the right decision. You have stated the problem as simply as you can. You have asked for guidance. " Before they call I will answer, and while they are speaking, I will hear."

There is no computer conceived by man that works with the same speed and efficiency. You will know what to do. All indecision will vanish. The still, small voice that speaks direct to your soul from the infinite source of all wisdom will speak to you. All you have to do is to give it the facts correctly, without distortion and provide the spiritual silence in which it can be heard.

The voice will not and cannot harm anybody. If your decision seems to do this, then be assured that you have not opened your inner self adequately and your selfish motives have been allowed to colour the moment. I am not suggesting that reason be set aside. What I am advocating is that you allow wisdom to illuminate your reasoning. This is the only way. It may take a little practice. It is worth it, I assure you.

Today we are surrounded by men of science, religion and technology whose minds are limited by the conviction that all that is to be known is already here. There are priests who are convinced that God exhausted His entire stock of spiritual knowledge two thousand years ago, and that any revelation man has received since is false. There are those who say that this happened five thousand years ago.

When I say to these men of religion that I, too, have had a revelation, that their old taboos and superstitions are wrong and misleading they shout, " Blasphemy." Yet it is they who blaspheme. Every day men receive their own guidance, divine revelations and spiritual replenishment. We need no synagogue, mosque or church to do this. God is everywhere and part of Him is in every one of us. It is they who blaspheme, conceiving God as a power-hungry and spiritually exhausted old man.

The scientists are not much better. When the aeroplane was first designed they said if God had wanted men to fly He would have given them wings. When the first steam locomotive was planned they said that if it travelled at more than twenty miles an hour it would arrive with coach loads of dead passengers, since the human body could not stand the strain. When the first steamship crossed the Atlantic it carried thousands of copies of scientific pamphlets " proving " that no steamship could reach America because the fuel needed would be more than it could transport.

The doctors are even worse. They have closed their eyes irrevocably to the power of spiritual healing. Every day thousands of people turn to healers for relief from diseases that orthodox medicine cannot cure. And many find robust and bounding good health after they have been told their ailments are incurable. Yet the British Medical Association not only denies that spiritual healing can heal. It threatens to have struck off the medical register any doctor who co-operates in any way with a healer.

Be warned. There is a natural law that operates against such people. It seems that whenever a man or woman shuts the door on spiritual truth because of materialism, lust, pride, prejudice, or arrogance, it stays closed. That man or woman is denied true wisdom. Only when a man opens his heart, puts aside the narrowness of orthodoxy and looks at himself and the world around him with a mind uncoloured by these prejudices will the door be opened.

Perhaps you have a problem at this very moment. Let us seek the truth together. Put down this book. Wherever you are, close your eyes. Seek to be still and quiet inwardly. In your mind state your problem. Then ask for wisdom to deal with it. There is only one qualification. You must ask for and seek only the truth. And when you hear the small, true voice telling you the truth, accept it.

Supposing you had a verbal agreement with a man to share equally in the proceeds of a sale. Perhaps you were selling some items of furniture you owned jointly. You have a list of the items. Against each is the price you both expected to realise. One item is a small, unframed oil painting. Against it is £10. A dealer in paintings offers you £100.

What should you do? You could accept the money and give your partner half. You could accept the money and tell him it was sold for £10, and give him half of that. You could get a friend to buy it as your nominee for £10, give your partner £5, and then get your friend to tote it around the galleries to see how much more you could make on it.

Of course, you could tell the dealer you had a partner to consult, ask him to come back when you had done so, tell your partner the full story and work out together what you should do. The course of action you should adopt is clear in this simple example.

But how many times have you made excuses for doing something that deep within yourself you knew was wrong? The psychiatrists call it " rationalisation." What it amounts to is the thought processes and internal arguments you devise to convince yourself that a wrong action is a right one.

I will not list any more examples. Think back on the last action you took about which you were less than content. Then remember the excuse you made to other people and, worst of all, to yourself.

This book is a do-it-yourself book. It has how-to-do-it in the title. Therefore, it will not succeed if those who read it cannot do it. I try not to preach. I try not to use fancy words. That is not because I doubt your ability to understand them. But because I want you to enjoy this book, to refer to it readily whenever you need help, and for it to have the widest practical use.

You may feel that in dealing with your daily problems you do not need wisdom. Perhaps simple common sense will get you through. Why use wisdom? Isn't it rather like opening a nut with a safe-breaking kit? I am not sure it is.

Wisdom permeates our everyday life. It is as necessary to condition our attitude towards quarrelsome neighbours as it is to deal with the problem of a delinquent teenager. Generally when people are perplexed they want to know if what they intend to do is right or wrong. In essence that is what any decision is about.

You may think that this is over-simplification. It is not. The most sophisticated computer in the world can make only one decision, " Yes " or " No." It can deal only arithmetically with two numbers, " o " and " 1." Yes, this is correct. The circuit of any computer can only, in its elements, pass or stop the flow of current. It is a yes-no machine.

It may be able to make thousands of these decisions each second. It may deliver a result in a few minutes that would take a man with a sheet of paper and a pencil weeks to calculate. But every computer programmer must recognise that he has to write the programme on a strictly " go-no-go " basis.

Sometimes we could profitably take a lesson from this simple fact. Too often we complicate our problem with side issues that are not relevant to the main decision. Suppose you ran a company and that business was very bad. Eventually you are faced with a decision. You have a thousand shareholders. They have invested their savings in your company. If you put the company into liquidation they will get nothing. The assets are just enough to pay off the creditors who have priority. You are the chief of these.

You have to make a decision. Put the company into liquidation and you get your money back, but the thousand small investors receive nothing. Pay off the small investors and you are left with a company that has insufficient assets to pay you. What to do? The accountant is advising you on immediate liquidation. The small shareholders are appealing to you to repay their investments. You have to make a yes-no decision.

Every day you have to make yes-no decisions. You have a mind that is more complex than the biggest computer. It has extensive memory banks and an amazingly interlinked circuitry. It also has an aid that no computer possesses. It can link to the source of infinite wisdom.

If you were running a big business and you had a modern computer to deal with administrative problems, you would use it whenever you could. But if you were a successful business man you would know that there were times when decisions had to be made based on your own concept of right and wrong.

I remember listening to a television interview given by Jim Slater. He runs a City firm of merchant bankers. He started eight years ago with £2,000. Today it is worth £99 million. He made this enormous amount of money by cool, analytical thinking. He said that when he came to deal with people he was ruthless in execution but compassionate in action.

If, for instance, he had taken over a company and found that a sales manager was inefficient, he would remove him without delay. The success of the company and the future livelihood of thousands might depend on the right man being put in his place, and fast, too. But he would immediately compensate the man he had removed by finding him a job in the group more suited for his needs, or retiring him on full pension a year or two before his time, or giving him generous compensation.

The decisions you have to make can always be helped by being able to link with wisdom. The answers are invariably clear and surprisingly often are on the yes-no basis. And remember that if an action is morally and spiritually right it cannot be wrong at any level.

It may be that you cannot see all the repercussions of your action. There may be times when doing what you know to be right might initially look to be commercially wrong. Do not doubt. A right action always brings right results.

There is a pattern to your life. It is complex. Your job is to do your best to discern that part of the pattern you can see and to conform to it. You are like a traveller journeying through a fascinating but sometimes dangerous territory. You have to keep to a narrow path. It winds through rolling countryside, swamps and quag-mires.

Sometimes the way is flat and easy going. Some-times it is mountainous and there are dangerous drops at the side of the road. Sometimes the path you are to take is clear and well defined. At others it is worn and obscured in mists. But it is there. You have only to seek it a little harder.

From time to time the path forks. You are undecided which way to go. The path to the left seems to lead to sunshine. The one to the right is shrouded in mists and rain. Which? On this journey you have a compass to guide you. It is called your conscience. To make it indicate the right way all you have to do is to ask it truthfully to let the small, clear voice talk to you. When it does, follow it without pause. The path it indi-cates may seem to lead into the mists. Follow it nevertheless. It is the only way.

Chapter 10

SEXUAL MATURITY

I T is not possible to write a book about how to be healthy, wealthy and wise without dealing with the question of sex. In fact it would be wrong to do so. The sex act, and the pleasure and feeling of well-being it brings, is an important part of our physical and mental health.

There is no such thing as a truly unprejudiced person. We are all the products of our education, environment, heredity and our experiences in life. Please put aside for the moment your prejudices and preconceived ideas about sex. Let us try and look at it from a fresh angle.

The first thing I want you to accept is that there is no norm in sex. The variations in appetite, fantasy, psychological needs and physical and mental attitudes are as many as there are people. What you call "normal" in sexual practice is what you regard as normal for yourself. It will not represent normality for anybody else.

The variations in sexual practice in time and place are infinite. For instance, when missionaries

started to visit the Pacific islands, they began to
teach their ideas as to how man and woman should
consort. The natives roared with laughter. Even
today they still regard the position of coition with
the woman on her back and the man above her
as inefficient, uninteresting and amusing. They
laugh when they talk about " the missionary
position."

Perhaps the best way of clearing our minds of
prejudice would be for us to take a cool look at
the sex scene in other civilisations. The idea of
monogamy is recent. In prehistoric times and for
years afterwards promiscuity was the general rule.

I suppose that most of us tend to look upon
Moses as the man who started our civilisation.
After all, his Ten Commandments are recognised
as the foundation of Western law codes. But five
thousand years ago when Moses was leading a
slave population into the wilderness, and trying
to forge a sense of nationalism into this nomadic
band of goatherds, the civilisation of China was
already old.

They had an alphabet, had invented gun-
powder (and had the intelligence to restrict its
use to making fireworks), had organised a large
and efficient civil service and had produced a
number of great poets and playwrights. Three
thousand years ago they had perfected the spinning of silk, had invented the process of making

fine porcelain and had started the widespread printing of books. They had produced some great philosophers, such as Confucius, and had developed a mature outlook on life.

The ancient Chinese views on sex were honest and simple. Sex was part of the natural enjoyment of our bodies. Like any enjoyment it tended to pall if it was overdone. And like any other pleasures it needed practice and some study to get the most out of it. A man took a wife. She gave him pleasure, and he reciprocated.

Confucius taught that life is a series of duties. The wife looked after the home, produced children, saw that her husband was well fed and happy, organised the servants and generally performed all the normally accepted functions of a matron. The husband, whilst pleased to have such a dutiful wife, sometimes found his sexual needs insufficiently supplied. So he took a second wife. She was younger and more active in bed. In her spare time she helped the first wife.

In time the second wife had children and became busy in the household. The man could then have a third wife, or take some young girls into his household as concubines. And if he needed a refreshing change from time to time he could go into the town and visit one of the lovely " singing girls."

Men, women and children had their duties to

one another, to the family and to the community. Subject to this, they enjoyed their bodies naturally and honestly, but with good taste and some natural modesty.

In ancient Greece they worshipped the beauty of the human body. Bodies were meant to be enjoyed. Young boys displayed their athletic prowess in front of large and admiring audiences. The boys wore no clothes. The young girls wore only a simple and revealing garment slit almost to the waist.

There was no prudery or shame. Rather they gloried in the beauties of their bodies. It was natural then that physical sensuality was uninhibited and the full enjoyment of heterosexual and homosexual practices was a normal part of their daily lives.

In India, too, there was no shame in the full exploration of sexual pleasure. The Indian considered that this was an enjoyment worth cultivating. There was a manual of sexual etiquette, the Kama Sutra. It may seem a little stylised today, but much of what it advocated is still sound practice.

One of the best selling books in America was a book about etiquette by Emily Post. Americans wanted to know how to behave in company so as to get the most out of their improving standard of living. Etiquette in India was more formal than in America. But they also thought that knowing how to act in bed was just as important.

Although there was no exchange of ideas on this subject, their attitudes were not so very different from those living in Japan. There, sex was regarded as part of the fabric of human experience. It was right to explore it to the full. Sex was pleasurable. It was fun. Not to enjoy it was stupid. You might as soon refuse to enjoy good food, a pleasant flower arrangement or a well-painted scroll.

A man took a wife because he wanted children, a partner to run his household, a woman to share his life and old age. But if he wanted a meal that was different from his home cuisine he went to a restaurant. And if he needed a change of sexual menu he went to bed with a girl or two.

There was no shame in sexual enjoyment, nudity, or in any form of natural pleasure. Today, the Japanese still have communal places where men and women bathe together in the nude. It is surprising how quickly the visiting European adapts to this pleasant custom.

What the Kama Sutra was to the Indian so *The Perfumed Garden* was to the Arab. It was a book that told about sex, how to do it, how to enjoy it, what was expected of you, how to prepare and behave in different circumstances. And very useful it was too.

The Arab recognised that monogamy had certain advantages in a small community where there were equal numbers of men and women. But it was an ideal almost impossible to attain. So he practiced polygamy as a concession to his needs and to the social demands on his first wife.

He looked upon sex simply as a natural and recreational pleasure to be enjoyed by all.

Moses had a problem. He had on his hands a wandering group of ex-slaves. He had to try and make them into some semblance of a nation. They needed to be toughened, to have the servile attitude of slavery bred out of them, to develop a fierce nationalism and pride, to become fighters, not servants.

In a land largely barren and in a climate that was at times a danger to health (since they lacked the benefits of refrigeration) he appreciated to the full the enormity of his task. He needed a set of laws to keep this mixed group of nomads healthy, free of internal strife and able to build together a sense of community.

Even with these harsh and largely negative laws it took forty years. Moses could have led the Israelites out of the desert whenever he desired. A map of their wanderings shows them going round in circles for forty years. It took him some time to mould a tribe of slaves into the fierce desert fighters the Israelites needed to become in order to survive.

The Jewish ideas on sex were, therefore, based on these needs. They wanted to promote the family as the basic social unit in their new tribal hierarchy. Their laws and regulations became obsessed with legitimacy. They still are. Adultery, in Jewish law, was defined as an act between a woman and a man who was not her husband. A man could not commit adultery. It was a female crime, because as a result she might produce an illegitimate child. And this was unforgivable.

Subject to this obsession, the Jews lived a full and active sexual life, regarding it as one of the God-given pleasures. It is even reported that Moses went on being sexually active until he died at a great age. It became the usual practice for an old man to find warmth, comfort and memories of his youth in the body of a young girl.

There is in the Amazon a tribe of natives who practise a system of marriage and sex control that makes the word "savages" seem singularly inappropriate. When a young man reaches the age to take a wife he goes to the chief of the tribe. The chief considers his nature and his capabilities and arranges a marriage to a middle-aged widow. The boy gets an established home, a good cook, an experienced lover and all the mothering he needs.

In this secure and happy environment he is introduced to the practices and art of the sexual act and learns to enjoy to the full the sensuality of his own and his wife's body. In time the wife dies, since she is older than her husband. He then goes to the chief and requests a new wife.

The chief chooses a young and attractive girl. She finds herself married to a mature and experienced man, introduced into a well-maintained and established house, and enjoying all the advantages of a controlled and very experienced lover. She has the father figure she needs. He, for his part, finds his middle and old age brightened by a younger and responsive girl.

When he, in turn, dies she goes to the chief, as a mature yet still young widow. He gives her in marriage to a robust and lusty young man to lighten her middle and old age. What a delightful arrangement! I am told it works very well indeed.

There was a maker of tents called Saul. He travelled widely in later years. Certainly he knew the harem ethics of the Arab countries. He went to Southern Europe, the Greek Isles, to Asia Minor, Italy and Spain. He was an epileptic and a misogynist. He did not get on well with women. Some historians say he was impotent. Others have suggested he was a homosexual.

This was the man who became known as St. Paul and responsible for the sexual laws of the

Christian religion. Christianity alone amongst all religions regards sex outside marriage as a sin.

Physical love, it teaches, is evil. Lust is the cause of birth, therefore human existence itself is sinful. Sex is not just the healthy enjoyment of our bodies. It is the most serious of moral wrongs, a trap fraught with ritual and personal dangers.

The indices of good, it asserts, are celibacy, virginity, marital fidelity in thought and deed, and the avoidance of nakedness. Christianity introduced shame into our enjoyment of the sex act. And from this sprang guilt.

The Church has used sex deliberately to generate anxiety as a method of maintaining its authority over the souls of men and women. No pornographer has ever exploited sex so thoroughly. Dr. Alex Comfort, in his authoritive book, *Sex in Society,* writes, "The fact of having made sex into a problem is the major negative achievement of Christendom."

The attitude of the Church, particularly as demonstrated by the revivalist type of preaching, has caused untold misery and an enormous amount of mental illness. Most of the mental illnesses in the Western world, most of the breakdown of marriages and personal relationships, most of the unhappiness can be traced to the guilt, insecurity, frustrations and the pressures from the teachings of the Christian Church.

The Arab regarded monogamy as the unattainable ideal and polygamy as a concession to physical needs. The Christians took celibacy as the ideal and treated monogamy as the concession to the demands of the flesh.

As a practising healer I get many patients suffering from the guilt and repressions of their religion-orientated education. The illnesses from which these people suffer are real. They may be emotionally induced, but they can hurt and disable as much as any physical damage. Amongst the conditions that I have met caused by these reactions are ulcers, stomach growths, migraine, fibrositis, arthritis, heart disorders, high blood pressure, back ache, chronic indigestion, asthma, sinusitis, skin eruptions and cancer.

When I asked you at the start of this chapter to clear your mind of all your prejudices about sex I did not expect you completely to succeed. But I hope you have now come part of the way along the road. Perhaps I could now replace those negative thoughts with some positive facts.

Sex is not wrong in itself. It is a natural and pleasurable function of the human body. The sex act should not be associated with guilt or shame. Our bodies have evolved in such a way that we can enjoy the exquisite pleasure of sensuality. We would be foolish not to do so. You could even say that the power to experience this enjoyment is a gift we have. To deny the gift is to deny the Giver.

I am not too fond of the philosophy that says if God had meant us to fly He would have given us retractable undercarriages and overnight bags. But I do feel that since we have been given these bodies we would be silly not to use them to the full.

Sex is not harmful. The male and female genitals have been designed to be used. Using them can do no harm. Nor can we use them to excess. There is no norm, therefore there is no excess. Except in extremely rare cases of physical deformity or malfunction, men and women get exhausted and have to sleep long before the continued sex act can do the slightest harm. The wear and tear are negligible. Our powers of recuperation are magnificent. As Emile Zola wrote, " Enjoy thyself." Go on, enjoy thyself.

The young explore their bodies in order to learn more about them. Masturbation and sex play are normal. Nearly everybody has done it. Even in adult life it provides a natural release of tension when other methods are not available. Because of the teachings of the West based on the sex regulations the Church imposed, masturbation has always been regarded as evil. This is nonsense. But the harm this doctrine has done can be measured by the preponderance of mental illness based on guilt syndromes.

In one orphanage in America some research was done which I have noted, but not condoned. There, the boys were not restricted in investigations of their bodies. Nearly all of them masturbated at some time or another. This was known but went unremarked upon. The boys were divided into two classes. Class A had religious instruction from which sexual references were omitted. Class B were subject to the full revivalist type of Christian teaching.

Both classes were followed into adult life and investigated in later years by welfare officers. Every member of Class B had had some type of mental illness or had to enter a mental home. None of Class A had any of these illnesses.

Marriage is a convenience. We practise monogamy because there are nearly the same number of men as there are women. If we lived in a community where there were six women to each man, polygamy would be the natural solution. And if we were in a group where there was a great shortage of women, then each wife would have several husbands.

Whether you are married in a church, synagogue or chapel makes no difference unless you believe your promises more binding on you personally. If you are married in a registry office you are merely complying with the rules and regulations of your community. What you have done is to assume the legal responsibilities that your country imposes on married people. If you live together you may avoid the legal responsibilities, but you might assume stronger and more spiritual ties.

The criterion of behaviour in sexual matters is your motive. If your motive is honest enjoyment with a partner who is free to share the enjoyment with you, this cannot be wrong. If your motive is to give enjoyment to your partner then this is all good. If two people love one another and want to express this in the sex act, then they have discovered one of the greatest manifestations of human relationships.

Premarital sex is a natural and healthy learning about our bodies. It should be done in the open and honest way that existed before the doctrine of Saul the Tentmaker. But watch two things. First, your motives must be good. If you are aiming to corrupt, then it is wrong. If you are sharing the enjoyment of sensuality with somebody who is a happy and freely united partner and you have no other motivation, then there is no harm in this. Secondly, try and achieve moderation.

The young have a very strong sex drive. It can exhaust them physically. It can override their needs. The young need to learn, study, acquire academic and professional status, investigate the enjoyment of art, music and the many means of expression that civilisation holds out to them To become obsessed with sex is like the man who cultivates one rose and ignores the rest of his garden.

Nor is extra-marital sex necessarily a bad thing. People have vastly different sexual appetites. A man may truly love his wife, yet she may have a low sexual appetite whilst he may have a high one. Perhaps in spite of all their efforts, he remains frustrated.

There are three alternatives. The first is to exercise control. That is what we have been taught. The man should "mortify the flesh." He should bottle up his feelings and learn to go without sex. This is the sort of advice you might expect from a priest who is celibate and sexually totally inexperienced. That a religion should have such sexual control over its adherents, and put in charge of this method of disciplining a man totally ignorant of it, never ceases to amaze and disgust me.

The second alternative is to have a divorce. Get married to another partner who is more compatible in bed. But the man truly loves his wife. He does not want a divorce. He wants her as his wife, as the mother of his children and the woman with whom he wants to spend his life and his old age.

The third alternative is to seek sexual relief and enjoyment elsewhere. In another society he would take a second wife or have a concubine. In Western society he is forced into a secretive and less satisfactory arrangement.

I cannot sit in judgment on such a man. The third alternative seems the only viable one. Rather would I sit in judgment on the society that puts him in the position of having to act in an underhand way.

I do not favour promiscuity. It is generally evidence of immaturity. In all things it is the wise man who makes sure that he controls his appetites. If you drink too much you can become an alcoholic, a sorry caricature of a man. If you become addicted to any other drug you are likewise giving away the ability to regulate your life.

The woman who eats too many chocolates, the man who smokes too many cigarettes, the man or woman who sleeps with a different partner several times a week—these are people who have let their appetites over-influence them. Whatever you do, keep in control. Try as many permutations as you like, but do so in moderation. Do not become addicted to sensuality. It is as dangerous as any other addiction.

There has been much controversy amongst religionists concerning contraception. The facts are simple. When the seed in a woman is fertilised the spirit entity enters the new life. For a time the contact is tenuous. But every hour sees it strengthened. It is conventional to regard the moment of birth as when the baby leaves the mother's womb and takes its first breath. But the child is then already nine months old. At that moment it changes from a creature drawing its oxygen supply through the blood to one who breathes through the lungs.

But before birth it lives. It can be seen in an X-ray picture. You can hear its heart beat. The prevention of the act of fertilisation is not wrong. It does not prevent a birth that was destined to take place. If such was its destiny then the contraception would fail. The full enjoyment of the sex act becomes more uninhibited and thus more pleasurable to men and women when the fear of pregnancy is removed. But whilst contraception is not wrong, abortion is.

The medical profession will in certain circumstance destroy a human foetus that is two, three or four months old. Abortion has reached such a level of general acceptance that it is regularly used as the final method of contraception.

In the special care wards in maternity units the doctors have succeeded in keeping alive a baby born three months prematurely. Their experience and research are progressing. Soon it will be accepted that a baby born four or even five months prematurely can have a good chance of survival.

What is happening is that the gap between the age at which a human foetus can be destroyed or helped to live outside the mother's womb has narrowed. Soon the gap will disappear. We are even now almost at the time when abortion cannot be regarded as the final contraception. It will be simply killing a baby that has a good chance of survival.

It is an amazingly short step to making positive instead of negative decisions. If a baby is not to survive because it is not wanted, or because it does not measure up to a pre-ordained genetic standard, then why not prevent the mating of parents? And who decides the standard? Who applies it? Who plays God?

What I have written in this chapter may upset some established ideas. To live a life that is healthy, wealthy and wise we all need to rid ourselves of the taboos and the superstitions. We all need to shed the inhibitions, ignorance and guilt.

As we progress and develop spiritual maturity so we appreciate that with this comes responsibility. The enjoyment of a full and happy sex life is the right of everyone. But see that your motives are pure, that you harm no man or woman, that you corrupt no child, that you exercise the powers of moderation your responsibility dictates. In sexual matters, as in all things, it is up to you.

Chapter 11

ANY QUESTIONS

I do not know all the answers. I do not even know all the questions. But as a practising healer I see a lot of people every week. Many of them are distressed. After they are healed they ask me questions. I have a large daily post. Many who write to me ask for guidance too. You could say that I have learned a lot from my patients. When you have regularly to give answers to problems of a spiritual, moral, psychological or physiological nature you make pretty sure of your replies.

Now that you have read this far, you probably have a lot of questions too. Perhaps I can anticipate some of them. Please forgive me if I do not deal with your particular problem. Perhaps if you read through this book again you may find the answer.

By now you should be a little better informed about yourself. You are, I am sure, on the way to wisdom. I hope you will not be hurt if I quote a proverb in defence of myself, " A fool can ask more ——ns in an hour than a wise man can answ—— —ven years."

Now you are —— fool and I am not a wise man. I merely —— this to excuse myself for not knowing all —— —wers. These questions are in no particular —— They are merely those that people ask m— I explain to them the various aspects of —— at are covered by the chapters of this bo—— —e first question I get asked more than any —— one.

Are my troubles, —— —s, or ailments a punishment?

No, they ar— —— —e the results of three separate causes. —— —his world is an education. You are here —— to evolve spiritually. You will survive this life. From it you will learn many things. The troubles you have are some of the tests you are set to see what you make of them.

Patients sit on my healing stool and start their histories by saying, " I have had a very worrying life." Here I stop them. " You have had problems," I point out, " and you have worried about them." Worry is one of your reactions to problems. It is your attitude to life that matters. The three separate causes are, first, the tests you are set as part of your educational course; second, your reaction to the circumstances that are presented to you; and thirdly, the way your body has reacted to a lifetime of wrong attitudes. No, you are not being punished. But you are unnecessarily punishing yourself!

Will I be punished after I die?

No, you will not. But you will have to answer for every deed, word or thought in this life. There is no Day of Judgment, no big book, no court of angels presided over by an elderly, bearded gentleman in a long, white nightshirt. Once you have adjusted to the change called death and have settled down in the next world, you will take a long cool look at the life you led in this one. You will sit in judgment on yourself. Nothing will be hidden. You cannot hide from yourself. The life you have just completed will be reviewed in detail.

When you have considered all the bad, foolish and good things, you will make a decision. You will have your guides to help you. They are what old books called " angels." The word comes from the Greek. It means messenger or guide.

You may decide you have not benefited much from this life. You will have to lead a new one. This means you must reincarnate. Or you may decide you have learned the lessons well and you are now ready for a higher plane of existence.

the spiritual awareness that was his. Often he was a healer.

When he died he was followed by lesser men. Gradually the psychic methods gave way to temporal authority. A set of rules was made. A dogma was contrived. A new religion was created.

Jesus, for instance, was an orthodox Jew. He was probably swarthy, Arab in appearance and dark-skinned, a coloured man perhaps. His spiritual awareness followed the pattern of many who had preceded him. He was not a God, but the son of man. He did not found Christianity and remained an orthodox Jew all his life. Christianity was the invention of other men.

Whether you believe the Bible stories to be true or not is up to you. If you want to do some research you may be surprised at the evidence against the claims of the orthodox. But through the Bible, as through all great religions, runs the golden thread of truth. This is the philosophy of love and service to others, the brotherhood of man and the survival of the human spirit.

Divorce the sound and true philosophy from the taboos, dogma, rituals, superstitions and the whole reward-and-punishment syndrome that has kept generations in chains and you end with a simple design for living that works, and with a system of belief that sees you through all your daily problems. Whether you are a Christian, Jew, Hindu, Moslem or a Taoist, this applies.

The revelations of different men varied in time and in place. Often they sought to suit the environment or the ethnic characteristics of their followers. But these men taught the same truths, because their revelation came from the one source.

I never go to church or any other place of worship. To me they are monuments to man's self-importance. They are architectural cenotaphs, cold, dead, obsolete, the abandoned air raid shelters of the war that never happened. I am a deeply religious person. To me religion is the blending of my spiritual and temporal life that allows me in the middle of this materialistic world to serve as a link between the less aware and the source of life itself.

Am I responsible for others?

No person is responsible for the spiritual evolvement of any other person, not even your own children. You may have two sons. One may be an evolved spirit who is far ahead of you along the road to spiritual awareness. He may be a great philosopher, sage, or a holy man. The other may have a young spirit that is immature. He may be hardly aware at all of his spiritual life and happy in his work as a slaughterman.

You are responsible for seeing that your children have a happy home life, are well fed and clothed, decently housed, kept warm and dry and given all the love and care they need. You should also see that they get the best and widest education they can absorb, and that they are not brainwashed into any sect or orthodoxy.

The only other responsibility you have is to show them a superb example. There is only one person for whom you are fully and completely responsible. That person is YOU. In the end, all the excuses, alibis, self-justifications and illusions you have created are swept aside. You are responsible for every act, thought and word you utter. There is no way of avoiding personal responsibility.

What should I eat?

I have known men who will drive six or seven miles out of their way to put a specific brand of petrol in the tank of their car. They believe the car runs better on this brand of fuel, wears longer and suits the motor better. This is nonsense. Subject to your choosing one of the many reputable makes of petrol of the right octane rating, there is no difference in the performance or wear of your car. Consumer testing has proved this without any reasonable doubt.

Yet the same man will then pull into the car

park of an hotel and promptly fill his personal tank (his stomach) with a load of adulterated rubbish that will result ultimately in the malfunction of his motor and in undue and excessive wear. The things people eat never cease to amaze me.

An animal bred for slaughter is kept under conditions that promote quick growth. These conditions may be against nature, cruel and devised only to exploit it so as to give the greatest material profit to the owner. The animal is fed on chemicals and drugs. Pellets of other drugs are implanted under its skin. When it has achieved its maximum growth it is driven to the slaughterhouse and there, in a state of fear and horror, killed.

The warm body is cut up, often still twitching with the last residue of life. The pieces of body are quick-frozen and left in store.

Some time later, years if needs be, parts of the animal are thawed, treated with one of the authorised red dyes so that the meat looks fresh, beaten with a mallet to break down the fibres to make it tender and saturated with chemicals to improve the taste. It is then cooked and served to a man who eats it under the impression he's doing himself some good. The extent to which animals are exploited for personal greed is appalling. It is an indictment of man's inhumanity.

It is not meat alone that is so treated. The so-called convenience foods are chemicalised, processed, refined, coloured and altered so as to have a doubtful nutrient value. You have only to read the small print on the package to see the wide range of chemicals that today we call food.

I knew a man who was allergic to monosodium glutomate, who found that there was almost nothing in the larder at home or in the staff canteen at work that was safe for him to eat.

This is the analysis of a well-known biscuit: " Wheat flour, processed Cheddar cheese solids, cotton seed and soya oil, cornflour, cheese flavour, artificial flavour, salt, sugar, mono- and di-glycerides, egg yolk, baking soda, monosodium glutamate, butylated hydroxyani-sole, butylated hydroxytoluene, certified colour, proply gallate."

Even bright green apples, golden carrots, ripe purple plums and juicy pears displayed by your local greengrocer are suspect. Many of these fruits are the results of farming that uses chemical sprays and insecticides in enormous quantities to produce a crop that is profitable.

Wild life in the countryside is being destroyed wholesale by these sprays. It is claimed that they are harmless to humans, but this is not entirely true. We are absorbing enormous quantities of chemicals. Who is to say when the individual reaches the danger level?

So what do you eat? I have a large family. I

am the only one who does not eat meat. I sit down to a meal and watch my wife carve a chicken that to me looks like a baby. I watch the children eat it. They eat little calves, cows, pigs, ducks and geese, and I say nothing. I sit down to my plate of vegetables, salads, eggs or cheese and wonder when, if ever, one of them will profit from my example.

Many of modern man's ailments are caused by eating the wrong food. I believe that grain, fresh fruit and vegetables untouched by chemicals, nuts, eggs, cheese and milk, provide a healthy and balanced diet. There is no need to breed, farm, slaughter and eat animals.

One day the world's inhabitants will be vegetarians. Then our international food problem will be solved. But what you eat is, like everything else, up to you. It was Brillat-Savarin in *Physiologie du Gout* who wrote, " Tell me what you eat, and I will tell you what you are."

Should I drink and smoke?

Alcohol is a drug. It is a powerful tranquilliser. It is a drug permitted by law to adults. There has grown up around the taking of this drug various rituals, taboos, superstitions and self-delusions: " One for the road. He's a good chap, drinks his beer like a man. Another little drop won't do us any harm. Drop into your local. Beer is best. Make sure the Dubonnet she's drinking is yours."

The advertising is carefully orientated to keep up the illusion. If you are a girl and drink Martini you get a " butch " chauffeur in polished leggings and are driven around in your own speedboat. You are a man of the world if you drink a particular brandy, a success if you drink a certain brand of whisky, irresistible to women with a particular vodka in your hand, one of the boys with a pint of that beer, getting a lot of nourishment from another, and one hell of a lad with a large glass, three chunks of ice, two fingers of gin and a splash of you-know-who's tonic water.

The whole thing is one colossal confidence trick to get you more and more addicted to the drug alcohol. If the same technique was applied to cannabis there would be an international scandal.

Let us get the facts right. Alcohol is a drug. You can become addicted to it. It can do your body and mind a lot of harm. It is one of the greatest killers in modern society. It is a substitute for maturity. Some people think they cannot find happiness or live a full life without this drug in one of its many forms. Can you?

So much has been written about smoking that I will not add to it. It is enough to say that it is a dirty, expensive and harmful habit. It, too, is a killer whose toll is mounting daily. Smoking is an addiction that is difficult to break. You may enjoy it. If you could see what it is doing to your lungs you would be disgusted and feel revulsion. Instead of your lungs being clean and wholesome they are like a sewer. If you want to shorten your life, ruin your breathing apparatus and waste your money, it is literally your own funeral. You must by now know the facts. Whether you drink or smoke is, like all things, up to you.

Do I have free will or is my whole life mapped out for me?

Entire books, libraries of them, have been written on this subject. Are we pawns in the game, with every act and thought predetermined? Does our destiny stand there recorded, unalterable, whatever we do? In India you will find many who think this is so. The beggar sits in the gutter. He will do nothing to improve his lot. " It is written." In the West, too, there are many who believe that their fate is predetermined. One of the classic excuses for sexual intercourse is " we were fated to come together." Why such a pleasant experience should need an excuse is beyond me.

People reason that if we are all the object of a great and divine plan then it must encompass everybody, every animal, action and interaction.

It says in the Bible that not a sparrow falls yet it is known to God. So it is argued that since the plan is based on an omnipotent and all-seeing power there is nothing we can do to alter it. This is fate.

It is patent that this explanation is false. Nobody can persuade me that Hitler and his murder of six million people were divinely inspired. Nobody can convince me that the horrors of the Holy Inquisition, which made Attila the Hun seem like a benign despot, were part of a great design. And the Church, remember, has been responsible for over twenty million deaths (though in all fairness it took them longer, so that Hitler's murder rate per annum is still the higher).

Well, what is the alternative? If there is no predestination then we must have free will. Is the whole universe one great accident? Is there no design? Does it really matter whether I do good as long as I have a terrific time and enjoy myself? If I am here as the result of a genetic chance, who can tell me what to do and not to do? I must just be an opportunist and make the most of things. Whatever happens to the rest, I'm all right, Jack!

Neither of these two extremes is correct. There is a plan, there is a design. Whether you like it or not you are part of it. You were born a man. You are short, stocky, with pale blue eyes and dark brown hair. Your place and time of birth were predetermined. So were your bodily characteristics. Your spirit which is occupying that body is at a certain stage of spiritual evolution. You are here to advance it. The type of life you will lead and its length are predetermined. Whether you will be a cripple, a spastic, or an athlete with a splendid body is known. Whether you will have the brain of a genius or of a moron is known. The problems you will meet and the tests that will be set you are known.

Within this general framework you have free will. Life here is like a university course. You know when the course begins and when it ends. The start and finish of each working term, holidays, syllabus and the schedule of lectures you have to attend and books you have to read are all known. So are the tests you have to pass and the examinations for which you have to sit.

What you do with all this is up to you. Some will waste time, spend too many hours at parties, slack and do little work. Others will attend all the lectures, work hard and try to get through the course the best they can. Life is just like that. It, too, is an education. Within a general framework of time, place, genetic characteristics and environment, you have a large measure of free will. It is, as in all things, up to you.

Will I survive death?

Yes, you are immortal. So am I. So is everybody. The teaching that you need to conform to the rules of a religious sect to achieve eternal life is false. You have eternal life. You cannot get rid of it. You are in this world to further your spiritual evolution. You are not a body that contains a spirit. You are a spirit. The body you occupy is a vehicle, nothing more. When you make the great change we call " death " you will discard the vehicle, like a man who gladly sheds a worn-out overcoat at the end of a long winter when he feels the warmth of the sun of summer.

You may return here to live another life, since you may find your evolution not yet sufficiently advanced to continue to a higher plane. You may not. If the lessons here have been well learned you may pass on to a fuller life. It does not matter if you are a prince or a pauper, an athlete or a cripple, a genius or a moron, a gifted composer or a road sweeper. It is what you do with what you have that matters.

The equipment you have in the shape of your mind, brain and body is the result of your choice. You may pity the mongol child, but the spirit in that undeveloped body may be a mature one seeking the compassion and understanding only

that life can bring him. You may envy the millionaire, yet his wealth may be a critical test, to find
out if he is sufficiently evolved to be trusted with
the power of riches.

Can you prove I am immortal?

No, I can prove nothing. I do not ask you to
believe anything I write unless it measures up to
two criteria. First, it must make sense. Second, it
must be proven to *you,* to your complete satisfaction. I believe that I have met the first standard.
What I write does make sense. The second I can
never meet. You alone can set the level that will
convince you. No one else can do this.

Do not accept survival of death until it has
been proven to your complete satisfaction. In the
life of every man is given one or more opportunities
to find the truth. You will have this opportunity,
never fear. When your moment of revelation
comes, be ready for it, with an open mind and a
pure heart.

Yet I have missed one possibility. We may meet
in the next world, you and I. And if we do, I hope
you will have the decency to come to me and say,
" You were right!"

*   *   *

As I said, I get asked many questions. In this chapter I have answered a few. I hope that in the preceding chapters I have answered some others. You must build your life on a sound foundation. If the materials are poor, the workmanship shoddy and the footings on shifting soil, then you must start again. The past is finished. Forget it, but remember the lessons it taught you.

". . . As in a building
Stone rests on stone, and wanting the foundation
All would be wanting, so in human life.
Each action rests on the foregoing event,
That made it possible, but is forgotten
and buried in the earth."

                              Longfellow

CONCLUSION

THERE are certain fundamental laws of nature that cannot be changed. Basically this world operates on the cause-and-effect principle. What you do, how you act, your attitude to the problems that are set you and to the people you meet determine your temporal and spiritual progress. I believe that we were meant to enjoy full and radiant good health. Illness is a perversion, most of which is self-induced. I have given in this book a simple formula for keeping healthy, becoming wealthy and for applying it for the common good.

Remember at all times that every man is your brother. If he is black, brown or yellow, if he eats strange food, worships pagan gods, practises peculiar rites, thinks odd thoughts and applies different values, he is still your brother. He, like you, will enjoy immortality. The continuous existence of the human soul is a fact. And his soul continues, too. You are not responsible for him, for his thoughts, prejudices and actions. You are responsible for yours. The more mature you become the greater is the responsibility.

You can forgive a fool because he knows no better. It is less easy to understand why a wise man should act foolishly. Remember you are here to learn and to profit from the lessons. One day you are going to sit in judgment on yourself when you cannot hide a single act, thought or motive. Maybe you would rather not have read this book. Now that you know what to do there is no excuse for not doing it.

Finally, let me give you a prayer:

" God grant me the serenity to accept the things I cannot change, The strength to change the things I can, And the wisdom to know the difference."

WHERE THERE'S A WILL

Maurice Barbanell

Whoever you are, and wherever you may be, you can call to your aid the greatest powers in the universe. You can obtain strength to conquer every weakness and guidance for every problem. You were intended to have a rich, full life. Within you are the means to achieve it.

In this simply worded book, the author explains how you can become the master of the infinite possibilities within you. Contents include:

THE CHALLENGE
TURNING ON THE SWITCH
THE WILL TO LIVE
FEAR IS FUTILE
HELP FROM THE UNSEEN
THE GLORY OF LIFE

"I have been conscious of help from the unseen," says the author, "the source of all inspiration, for which I express my gratitude. I pray that some of the wisdom, which I have sought to capture, helps those who are seeking the way to a fuller life."